Nat is a comedian, rock musician, mental health advocate and award-winning, bestselling author. Already an online creator with a fan base in the hundreds of thousands for close to a decade, Nat's What I Reckon rocketed to global prominence when he took the world by storm in early 2020 with his isolation cooking content.

Nat's platform has enabled him to hold a tongue-in-cheek mirror up to antiquated cultural norms, to promote kindness and to share his battle with anxiety and depression, collecting him a dedicated audience of over 2.5 million thanks to his message of positivity and inclusivity that has resonated with champions the world over.

When he's not filming, cooking or foraging for rosemary, Nat can often be found indulging his love of rock'n'roll and comedy, playing in various bands and stand-up rooms around Australia (COVID permitting). His bestselling debut book, *Un-cook Yourself*, was shortlisted for General Non-fiction Book of the Year at the Australian Book Industry Awards and won the Booktopia Favourite Australian Book Award for 2020, the proceeds of which Nat donated to Beyond Blue.

natswhatireckon
@nats_what_i_reckon
natswhatireckon
natswhatireckon

NAT'S WHAT I RECKON

DEATH TO JAR SAUCE

RAD RECIPES FOR CHAMPIONS

Illustrated by Sydney artists Onnie O'Leary, Bunkwaa, Glenno and Warrick McMiles

EBURY PRESS

UK | USA | Canada | Ireland | Australia
India | New Zealand | South Africa | China

Ebury Press is part of the Penguin Random House group of companies
whose addresses can be found at global.penguinrandomhouse.com.

First published by Ebury Press, 2021

 A catalogue record for this
book is available from the
National Library of Australia

ISBN 978 1 76104 582 0

penguin.com.au

I dedicate this book to you,
champion.

Onya for giving cooking
a red-hot go.

CONTENTS

STUFF THAT GOES WITH OTHER SHIT

AFTER DINNER MINTS

G'DAY
CHAMPION

Death to Jar Sauce, eh Nat? What does that even mean? Is all food in jars now sin-binned for incidentally ending up in a cylindrical glass vessel?

Not necessarily, champion! The jar itself is not the issue; in fact, if you put the food in the jar yourself then you win ten points and get to come to my birthday party and we can be best friends 4eva. No: the title *Death to Jar Sauce* is a metaphorical fist in the air saying 'fuck that shit' in protest against boring-as-fuck instant pre-made garbage, and a high five to having a red-hot go at cooking awesome feeds yourself. Consider yourself invited to the protest/ party, champion.

I'm sure there're one or two of you out there thinking, Is this actually going to be a fucken cookbook this time or what, smart-arse? To be fair, I think what threw a few people off last time was that my first book had me holding a rubber toy fish and a knife on the cover above the words 'Un-cook Yourself', which gave off a vibe to some that it was gonna be a cookbook . . . which it was – in parts. But there was a fair bit of fucken prattle-on in there, too. Now I reckon I might do a cheeky 180 on ya here and give you an almost entire cookbook this time, but of course with heaps of other shit in here 'cause I can't leave tradition alone. And just 'cause I wanna, I've thrown in some unrequested opinion pieces on everything from microwaves to the trite discussion of pineapple on certain cheesy discs of baked dough. I wanna kinda go for a cookbook that you'd pick up even if you're not about to cook something, and maybe just wanna have a laugh or a froth over some cool drawings.

I have some powerful masters of the illustration world on board to help make this wild idea happen: Onnie O'Leary, Glenno and Bunkwaa from the last book, and this time we have an additional legend joining the gang, my mate Warrick McMiles. I reckon you'll dig their stuff big time.

I have gone with another possibly intense colour for book

number two. It was a fucken flog trying to decide on what colour was going to make the drawings of the food look awesome and not as though everything is mandarin flavoured, and not make me look like I have jaundice. I hope you're into this colour – if not, you're gonna be suffering in your jocks, friend, 'cause we are going flat chat with it.

I have had a wild fucken time since the last book came out, the bloody thing won the Favourite Australian Book Award for 2020, which is a fat spin-out. The only award trophy I ever scored prior to that is for participating in under 11s local football, so this has been huge news. Thanks gang. I've been getting mad extra on the awards ceremony energy, too. I've presented awards at the ARIAs, the Australian Book Industry Awards, *B&T* magazine's 30 Under 30, and loads of other shit, too. I've been a part of Download Festival in the UK, BIGSOUND in Australia – the over-achieving list goes on. Fuck, what a ride. I seriously thought I was doomed to being a metalhead burnout for the rest of my life. I am so stoked that so many legends out there are digging what I'm doing.

With all that said, if you've been given this book as a gift and straight up think it's a massive load of trash, you can always pull the old tried and true 're-gift' move. That is, of course, if you don't bend the pages too much and someone hasn't already written a lovely note on the front page for you.

I warn you about these things because I did it once and every time I think about it, it makes me fucken die inside.

The story goes, I wanted to give my mates something nice but I had no money and I hadn't read any of the books I'd been given, and, to be perfectly honest, I fucken wasn't going to. I also felt that as a broke teenager I wasn't chipping in enough to the friend group, so I gave each of them a book out of seemingly nowhere. But because I was a fucken 16-year-old dumbass, I didn't think to leaf through the first few pages and check if these about-to-be 're-gifts' had been signed. I simply handed over a book or two with heartfelt notes in them addressed to . . . that's right, yours truly. *Slaps forehead* Fucking hell!

See, we are already getting off track here, something I'm very good at.

Before we go any further I think we should address some of the unasked questions that no doubt some of you are likely to have about parts of the content in this recipe book.

For a start:

1. **'Why didn't you get a full colour book printed with photos of the food in it, Nat, ya bloody dickhead?'**
   Fantastic made-up question, thank you for asking. The reason is many reasons, one of which is that every normal cookbook more or less does that, and I am a misunderstood try-hard over here who insists on doing things differently.

2. **'Are there any vegan dishes in this book, you bloody maniac?'**
   Fuck yes there are, and even some li'l hacks to shift a recipe to the vego side of town. This is a book for all champions of all dietary persuasions . . . unless you're on that strange potato diet, then maybe not. Although you could check out my Get Fucked Roast Potatoes recipe if you do happen to be limited to that ingredient alone.

3. **'I'm concerned that there will be heaps of swearing in this book as well, because there's already been a tonne.'**
   Yes.

4. **'Are you even a real chef or am I just taking advice from some long-haired yahoo covered in stupid drawings?'**
   I'm glad you asked, Tim. No, I'm not a chef, but I do give an enormous shit about the food I create. I've put my money

where my mouth is more than a few times before. That's not to say I haven't occasionally bitten off more than I can chew (cooking joke there) and made a dish that looks and tastes nothing like what I set out to make. With that said, there will be none of that nonsense in this book, as everything here is nothing but rock-solid total wins that will leave you feeling like you've absolutely slayed the home-cooking game.

5. 'I don't have any more questions.'

Me either.

If you're someone who is slightly overwhelmed by the tidal wave of precious info in a lot of recipes, then this is the book for you. I suppose my lack of professional training has sometimes led me the long way around to nailing a few of these dishes, and as a result I've found out that a lot of stupid, unnecessary instructions in them don't make any fucken difference to the final dish. I've put in a lot of hours to this freestyle, so you don't have to. Also, I suppose that not a lot of cookbooks have drawings of the person who has written them dressed as the Terminator or a fish, so if you're chasing something a little different, chase no further, legend.

To add more unusual shit to the book I have created something called a Hectometer which is a kind of heads-up dial to give you a bit of a shout on how hectic each dish is to make.

easy AF

bit of a flex

So if you've had a big day and don't feel like being thrown in the deep end of the pool without a floaty, then this should help. But rest assured, there are no recipes in here that are too stressful, as I try to avoid stress in general and chip in for more good times than meltdowns.

So, champion, I hope you get a good laugh out of these recipes as well as feel like you've added a few new smash hits to your cooking repertoire. Maybe you'll play around with them a bit and make your own 'Sara-sagne' or perhaps the soon-to-be-famous signature 'Michael-andwich'? Who bloody knows? But I hope so. That's the cool thing about cooking recipes that other people have written and not being those people – you can crank a tonne more of your favourite shit in or add a herb or spice that you reckon would be a fucken winner to suit your tastes and expression session.

These are not hard-and-fast rules on how to make this food by any means, this here book is more about sharing some of my favourite dishes with you, and the ways I like to make them.

So let's get in the kitchen, crank the tunes, drop-kick the jar sauce over the back fence and rage some face-melting dishes that are sure to get some smiles on some dials.

KITCHEN SHIT I USE

have a few bits of kit in the kitchen that make cooking actually enjoyable and not a fucking flog. A handful of awesome tools can make a huge difference to whether you love or hate making a meal. Commercial cheffing shops often have cheaper shit sturdy enough to take a beating, so they're worth visiting if you have access to one near ya.

Here are my go-to pieces of equipment that save my arse in the kitchen time and time again:

1. A FUCKING SHARP KNIFE

The number one thing that makes life so much fucking easier, safer and adds such a huge amount of joy to your time in the kitchen is a sharp knife. You don't have to travel to the ends of the earth to find the perfect blade, nor do you need to sell your car to afford a decent one. The real name of the game is that it is sharp and you keep it sharp. A blunt knife does your head in while also being unsafe – surprisingly more than a sharp one, would you believe. Some are easier to sharpen than others. If you are looking for a good workhorse, spend a few bucks on a half-decent stainless or carbon steel chef's knife. If you decide to go for carbon steel, be warned that it takes a bit more tender loving care to maintain, but they are beautiful to use and sharpen easily. There is a whole book on what you're in for with one, so if you don't want to fuck around heaps, head for the stainless steel knife part of town, just be aware they are a hard metal and tougher to sharpen but tend to stay that way for a little longer.

Also, hot tip: don't throw your good knives in the second drawer down with all the other stupid shit, as this kind of behaviour is what sends it in the express post to the capital of Bluntville, banging around in there. And don't put it in the dishwasher either . . . just don't.

2. KNIFE SHARPENING GEAR

There are a zillion things out there that do the trick, the best of course is a sharpening stone and a steel, but if you can't be fucked with all that nonsense, there are loads of easy-to-use sharpening wheels and devices on the market to help keep your bad bois nice and sharp. Another hot tip is that your local butcher usually has a knife sharpening service if you can't be fucked with all that buggering around.

3. FAT WOODEN CHOPPING BOARD

Before I say anything, let me say I think glass chopping boards straight up should be banned. The clanging, banging noise alone when using one makes my hair stand on end while I die inside waiting for the thing to fucken smash. I love a big, heavy wooden one so it doesn't slide around like a fucking dickhead and give you the Jiminy Crickets. You can throw a tea towel or non-slip mat underneath if it's skidding about. A solid investment well worth the money. Super thin chopping boards tend to fucken warp after a while so I like the thicker ones.

When it comes to cleaning it, don't soak a wooden board in water unless you want to be cutting shit on a misshaped pain in the arse; a little warm water and soap and then stand to dry gets you out of trouble. Keeping it oiled with a little mineral oil stops the water soaking into the wood, too.

4. HALF-DECENT SET OF POTS AND PANS

I get away with using mostly a big frying pan or sauté pan with a lid, wok (remind me to buy one, pls), large stainless steel stockpot and a cast-iron casserole dish or Dutch oven. Again, you don't have to spend a tonne on this shit, as long as it's durable and can handle a bit of a workout. If you live in a share house then good luck with

Teflon. I use a mix of stainless steel and non-stick pots and pans, depending on what I'm cooking, but a good big non-stick frying pan is a reliable and simple-to-use piece of cookware that can make things a lot easier. Of course, don't use metal implements on the Teflon or you will scrape it off and end up eating it or killing the joyous non-stick sensation. Another no-no is heating up a Teflon pan too hot without shit cooking in it, as this can fuck up the non-stick surface and it's not amazing for the old lungs to breathe in either. A wok is also a ripper and very versatile piece of kit that doesn't just have to be for cooking stir-fried food. I swear by the huge stockpot, too. If you can score one, it comes in very handy for a tonne of different dishes. The cast-iron pot isn't totally necessary but it is a nice thing to have at your disposal. They stay nice and hot when you're cooking so are great for not losing heat when adding cool ingredients – keep an eye out for sick cheap ones.

5. FOOD PROCESSOR/ DECENT BLENDER/ STICK BLENDER

The food processor or a decent blender that can do a similar thing will help make quick work of otherwise lengthy chopping and blending a whole bunch of stuff at once. The stick blender is a killer for soups, sauces and even mayonnaise. It also saves you having to ladle hot shit out of a pot and back in when making soup.

6. WHISK

Just have one, though.

7. ELECTRIC BEATER

Unless you're on the gains train, then I recommend using one for a lot of baking stuff. Whipping cream is a flog without it.

8. DECENT GRATER OR MICROPLANE

A Microplane is the one-stop shop for grating and zesting and also awesome for shaving your skin off your knuckles if you slip.

9. A BUNCH OF STAINLESS STEEL MIXING BOWLS

Get all the sizes, they are cheap and help heaps. If you're like me and like to have all your shit in bowls ready to rock before you kick off, these will have your back.

10. A MICROWAVE

Just kidding.

11. MEASURING JUGS, CUPS AND SPOONS

'Cause measuring.

12. BAKING TRAYS

A good flat one and a nice big deep one are the shit for most stuff. Stainless steel is pretty great if you can find reasonably priced gear.

13. KITCHEN SCALES

Such a huge win. You don't need to fork out your life savings for one. Just so rad for helping to take the guess work out of stuff.

'A HANDFUL OF AWESOME TOOLS CAN MAKE A HUGE DIFFERENCE TO WHETHER YOU LOVE OR HATE MAKING A MEAL.'

14. SPICES

Get all the spices 'cause being a spicy pants is fun to play around with.

15. MORTAR AND PESTLE

Not only does it make you look like a real foodie nerd, a mortar and pestle is great for smashing seeds and herbs to bits and creating flavours that are out of this world. If your pepper grinder is a fucken piece of shit like mine, then the mortar and pestle takes charge easily. It's fun to play around with spices in it – highly recommended.

These are my faves that I use the most. Of course there are bits and pieces like wooden spoons, tongs, ladles etc., but I would fucken be here all day announcing everything in my kitchen if I did. You certainly don't need to have all this shit to make all the stuff in this book happen, but it definitely helps make life a little easier in the kitchen at the end of the day, and feeling stoked with some solid gear is a nice feeling when you go to create radness in the kitchen again.

WHEELIN', DEALIN' & MAIN MEALIN'

This dish is one of the most classic hits of all time. It can also be a classic bastardised punish if it's jammed with a tonne of stupid shit. God knows the signature bolognese recipe additions I've seen before have been nothing short of fucking bizarre, I've even made a few strange moves myself in the past – everything from barbecue sauce to Vegemite. Now, by all means, put whatever you want in your sauce, but the title of 'bolognese' loses its identity fast when ingredients like zucchini and capsicum enter the room. Made my way – I promise you a classic done right – it's like a good dance move you can rely on without landing on your arse in front of everyone.

SERVES: 6–8*

COOKING TIME: 1–however bloody long ya like hours

HECTOMETER: 4/10

* depending on how sauce heavy you go

INGREDIENTS

- 1 ONION
- 2 CARROTS
- 2 STICKS CELERY
- 150-200g PANCETTA (CAN SUBSTITUTE BACON)
- 25-30g BUTTER
- OLIVE OIL
- A BIT OVER 500g EACH OF PORK AND BEEF MINCE
- FRESH ROSEMARY, THYME OR OTHER SAVOURY HERB (OPTIONAL)

- GLASS OR 2 OF WINE (RED OR WHITE)
- 300g TOMATO PASTE
- 1 CUP MILK
- 1-2 CUPS CHICKEN STOCK
- SALT & PEPPER TO TASTE
- BAY LEAVES (WHO KNOWS IF THEY REALLY DO ANYTHING ANYWAY, SO LET'S PLAY IT SAFE AT 2-3)
- 500-750g PASTA (BUY SOME FUCKEN NICE BRONZE-EXTRUDED SHIT WOULD YA, THE COUPLE OF EXTRA BUCKS GOES A LONG WAY)

- PARMESAN, TO SERVE

HERE'S WHERE YOU CAN CHOOSE TO ADD SOME ROSEMARY. IF YOU LIKE, GO OUT AND PICK SOME, IT GROWS FUCKEN EVERYWHERE! JUST CHUCK IN THE WHOLE SPRIG, INCLUDING THE STALK. IF YOU PREFER TO USE ALTERNATIVE HERBS, GO FOR GOLD!

KEEP COOKING THE LIQUID OUT UNTIL THE MEAT MIX IS FRYING. ONCE THE LIQUID IS FRIED OFF ADD A GLASS OR TWO OF WINE.

THERE IS AN ARGUMENT THAT YOU SHOULD USE WHITE WINE OVER RED WINE BUT I'M NOT GETTING INVOLVED IN THAT ARGUMENT.

AGAIN, WITH THE QUALITY OF THE BOOZE, THAT'S UP TO YOUSE.

LET THE BOOZE COOK OFF FOR A COUPLA MINUTES THEN DROP IN YOUR TOMATO PASTE.

THERE ARE A FEW WAYS TO SERVE THIS BUT HERE'S HOW I LIKE IT:

DRAIN THE PASTA AND RETURN IT TO THE POT.

LADLE IN AS MUCH SAUCE AS YOU LIKE AND GIVE IT A KICK ROUND IN THERE. IF YOU SEE THE ROSEMARY STALK OR BAY LEAVES YOU CAN GRAB THEM OUT IF THEY BOTHER YOU, BUT DON'T FRET TOO MUCH, MUSCLES.

BUNG SOME MILK IN IT . . . DARE YA

Well, fuck me. Didn't the idea of putting milk in ya bolognese ruffle a few feathers, eh? I even ended up in the fucken newspaper over it, was asked about it on the news, and there were journalists asking well-known chefs for their two cents on the breaking issue. Some of the comments on my video were hilarious.

My wife has never complained about my bolognese sauce til now. Turns out I've been doing it wrong for the last 12 fucking years.

I could send you my recipe but somehow I think if you watch Nat you won't forget . . . not sure about milk though?

This is blowing my mind. Guess what's on the menu this weekend . . .

Just made it . . . milk and all . . . aaaand . . . it does not suck. Like at all.

I just made this version with milk and no zucchini (sorry just had beef mince and non-alcoholic red wine). My boyfriend said it was the best spag bol I've ever made.

Milk? You turn your nose up at zucchini but add milk??? I can't even imagine how that works <sigh> You haven't failed me yet, Nat, so I will give it a go.

It does! It really does!! We have made it this way before.

To be honest, I needed the zucchini lecture.

This guy is so good and knowledgeable. As an Italian person you have NO IDEA how gratifying it is to hear 'mushrooms do not go in bolognese' . . . I was almost moved for a second. 😄

Thanks for this Nat! Did a blind tasting of our regular bolognese vs End of Days, and End of Days won easily. It's the milk! I'd love a version of your channel with a soundtrack suitable for younger kids . . .

Never heard of using milk before and was a bit sceptical I won't lie, but being adventurous I gave it a crack, what a winner, champion 👍

You have solved a 22-year-old argument my husband has had with me over my spag bol cooking! OK I will now not include zucchini and mushroom ever again! Someone is smiling in this house.

That was, of course, until people tried it and were like, 'Shit, this is actually unreal'. It's not even my move, to be honest. As far as I know, the traditional recipe from Bologna has milk in it and there's a bloody good reason for that – because it rules. I'll be honest, the first time I heard it was a thing, I was a bit like, 'Wow, okay.' I love cooking the same thing over and over again until I get it exactly the way I like it, and bolognese is no different. When the milk made its way into my sauce for the first time it was fucken groundbreaking shit, I thought I'd found some kind of tasty holy grail.

I get that playing it safe when it comes to a few fundamental things isn't a bad idea, but let me tell ya, when it comes to bolognese, it's a classic hits thing, and when done right and not filled with a million loads of stupid shit from the arse-end of your fridge, it is magical stuff.

Sometimes ya just gotta throw caution to the range hood and try something new. It may even end up being your next favourite thing – so go on, then, fang in the milk and tell me it doesn't totally slay!

ME, MYSELF AND
GUINNESS PIE

There are few people on earth that love a pie more than Jules' dad, John. He takes this pie business very bloody seriously, and so he should. God knows we have all suffered many a shitty maggot bag from time to time, but if we are lucky enough we've also had the great fortune to experience a truly awesome pie that makes us reconsider all our previous servo dining moments.

When I discovered how fucking awesome it is to stew beef in Guinness, the words 'let's eat another pie' left my lips on multiple occasions, and I made a zillion of these fucken things until I got a heartburn so bad I just about burned down the house. Good news, though: I came good and now I'm ready to make the pie world proud with my own meaty frisbee full of all the flavour a mouth can hang with.

Let's eat like we mean it and not like we're filling up with E10.

SERVES: 6–8
COOKING TIME: a few hours
HECTOMETER: 7/10

INGREDIENTS

1.5 KG STEWING BEEF (CHUCK, BLADE, BRISKET)
2 TABLESPOONS OLIVE OIL OR VEGETABLE OIL, PLUS EXTRA IF NEEDED
1 LEEK
1 CARROT, PEELED
2 ONIONS, PEELED
ALL THE GARLIC IN THE WORLD (AT LEAST 1 WHOLE GARLIC BULB), PEELED
SALT & PEPPER
2 TABLESPOONS CHOPPED ROSEMARY LEAVES
2 BAY LEAVES
1/4 CUP TOMATO PASTE
1 TABLESPOON BROWN SUGAR
440 ML CAN GUINNESS OR STOUT
2 CUPS BEEF STOCK
2 TABLESPOONS WORCESTERSHIRE SAUCE
1/4 CUP PLAIN FLOUR
1 TABLESPOON BUTTER
2 SHEETS SHORTCRUST PASTRY
1 EGG, LIGHTLY BEATEN,
   FOR EGG WASH
2 SHEETS BUTTER-PUFF PASTRY

GEAR YA NEED

2-LITRE BAKING DISH

MICROWAVES

There's a lot to be said about the infamous tucker fucker. In their heyday, microwaves were all the rage with people mesmerised at the ease and speed of 'cooking' food in them. I understand that not wanting to fuck around taking ages to cook dinner is a lot of people's M.O., but does it really *cook* things? Yeah, I suppose it does, but it heats them up rather than truly cooks them. It certainly doesn't do the best job of cooking a decent meal, in my opinion. I'm fascinated by how fucked up some of the dishes are in microwave cookbooks, having made several myself on the channel.

That's not to say they are entirely useless; I think the tucker fucker has its place. I know a lot of professional kitchens rely on them to heat food up quickly, as do lots of us at home reheating shit, but my issue isn't so much with that use as it is with the entire cooking of a meal from the ground up. When I found out that people 'roast' entire chickens in them I just about had a cardiac arrest. The most famously overly trusted meal in the microwave universe in my opinion is the reheated meat pie. I covered this heinous shit in my first book, but truly, the microwaved maggot bag has to be one of the worst things to rear its boiled head from a microwave. It entirely defeats the purpose of having previously baked pastry. The evil magic of a microwaved meat pie really is that you are eating an all-at-once-scaldingly-hot-yet-kinda-still-frozen-in-parts meal that destroys any chance of having skin left on the roof of your mouth or of enjoying the flavour of whatever the fuck is in the thing.

I respect that it's not the 80s any more and things have changed, but I think reheating stuff in the tucker fucker – while it may not be my favourite way to go about it – is still fine. If you're cooking a fucken raw chicken in it, however, scrambling eggs or even, God forbid, attempting to cook fish in there, then I think I have to say **fucken 'yes' ... microwaves are shit.**

STRAIGHT TO THE
POOL ROOM
RISSOLES

When rissoles were on the menu in the movie *The Castle*, I felt like I'd time travelled back to a kitchen table moment in the early 90s that quite a few of us have very likely enjoyed – fond memories always! I'll even take a burnt one these days if there's enough sauce on it. Rissoles are a great way to turn a regular burger patty into a feed that is a little more dynamic than just having a burger for tea. If you take the time to keep working the ingredients into each other in the mixing bowl, then you will no doubt end up avoiding the common complaint of 'my fucken rissoles always fall apart'. Buckle up for a real old-school Aussie classic here, and a bloody good one, too.

SERVES: 4–6
COOKING TIME: under an hour
HECTOMETER: 3/10

PLONK!

INTO THE RISSOLE BOWL GOES THE RISSOLE MEAT. THEN GRATE IN YOUR CARROT, ZUCCHINI AND ONION. YOU CAN DO IT WITHOUT PUTTING YOUR BACK INTO IT, MR OLYMPIA. GENTLE PRESSURE WILL GET YOU THERE; IF WE WANTED IT THICK CUT, WE WOULD JUST DO THAT.

GET YOURSELF A BIG PINCH OF PARZZZLEY AND CHOP IT FINELY. CHUCK THAT INTO THE BOWL AS WELL, WITH YOUR GARLIC POWDER, ONION POWDER AND DRIED THYME. CRACK IN THE EGG AND ADD THE BREADCRUMBS, DIJON MUSTARD, WORCESTERSHIRE SAUCE, A BIG PINCH OF SALT AND PEPPER TO TASTE.

MR OLYMPIA

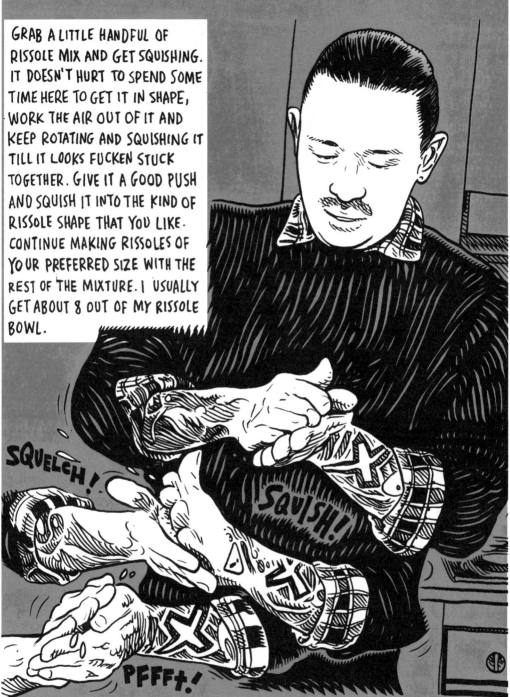

GRAB A LITTLE HANDFUL OF RISSOLE MIX AND GET SQUISHING. IT DOESN'T HURT TO SPEND SOME TIME HERE TO GET IT IN SHAPE, WORK THE AIR OUT OF IT AND KEEP ROTATING AND SQUISHING IT TILL IT LOOKS FUCKEN STUCK TOGETHER. GIVE IT A GOOD PUSH AND SQUISH IT INTO THE KIND OF RISSOLE SHAPE THAT YOU LIKE. CONTINUE MAKING RISSOLES OF YOUR PREFERRED SIZE WITH THE REST OF THE MIXTURE. I USUALLY GET ABOUT 8 OUT OF MY RISSOLE BOWL.

SQUELCH!

SQUISH!

PFFFt!

HEAT SOME OLIVE OIL IN A FRYING PAN TO MEDIUM-HIGH HEAT. LAY YOUR RISSOLES IN CAREFULLY AND COOK FOR A FEW MINUTES EACH SIDE OR UNTIL THEY ARE DONE. WATCH THE HEAT, HADES, AS TOO HOT AND THEY WILL LOOK LIKE A CUPPLA BRIDGESTONE TYRES.

IT'S A FUCKEN ALL-TIME BELTER THIS ONE. YOU CAN ADD AND REMOVE LOADS OF COOL SHIT IN RISSOLES SO GO EXPERIMENT IN YA LAB AFTER YOU'VE TRIED THESE. SERVE IT WITH SOME CLASSIC SIDES LIKE MASH AND ROASTED CARROTS, AND DON'T BE SCARED OF HAMMERING IT WITH YA FAV TOMATO OR BBQ SAUCE.

'GET READY TO
HIKE UP YOUR
FANCY PANTS
BECAUSE WE'RE
GOING FOR A MODEST
CANTER DOWN
TO FUCKEN RAD
FOOD MANOR.'

PULLED PORK TACO NIGHT

Taco night was always a very bloody exciting time for me as a kid. As a young fella, being able to choose my own adventure while filling a shitty, flimsy corn chip–style taco shell with sachet-seasoned mince and all the fucken cheese on earth was a truly bloody wild time. I've put away a lot of traditional Mexican food in my adult years, while living overseas, and omg it's fucken amazing stuff. The shit I've had from those fucken powdered flavour sachets here in Australia couldn't be further from those rad memories if they tried.

Side note: pulled pork is something everyone at pubs in Sydney has had a fucken fascination meltdown over during the last ten years. So why don't we try to channel the ravenous creativity and joy of being a kid at taco night, while also attempting to harness the obsessive gastropub pulled pork energy from a decade ago, and create something that gives us a way more righteous taco night and give sachet trash the bird.

SERVES: 4–6
COOKING TIME: about 3 hours
HECTOMETER: 5/10

INGREDIENTS

- 1.2–1.5 KG BONELESS PORK SHOULDER MEAT (SKIN REMOVED)
- 1 BROWN ONION
- 1 BUNCH CORIANDER, STALKS CHOPPED, LEAVES RESERVED FOR TACOS AND GUAC
- WHOLE GARLIC BULB
- 2 TABLESPOONS OLIVE OIL OR VEGETABLE OIL
- SALT
- 2 TEASPOONS CHIPOTLE POWDER
- 2 TEASPOONS SMOKED SWEET PAPRIKA
- 2 TEASPOONS GROUND CORIANDER
- 1 TEASPOON GROUND CUMIN
- 1 TABLESPOON BROWN SUGAR
- 2 TABLESPOONS TOMATO PASTE
- 400 G CAN WHOLE TOMATOES
- 2 CUPS CHICKEN STOCK
- 400 G CAN BLACK OR PINTO BEANS, RINSED AND DRAINED
- SOFT AND (IF YOU LIKE) HARD SHELL TACOS, SOUR CREAM AND SHREDDED CHEDDAR, TO SERVE

GUACAMOLE
- 2 AVOCADOS
- ½ RED ONION, PEELED AND FINELY CHOPPED
- 1 JALAPEÑO PEPPER, DESEEDED AND DICED
- 1 TOMATO, DESEEDED AND DICED
- HANDFUL CHOPPED CORIANDER LEAVES
- JUICE OF 1 LIME
- SALT

(OPTIONAL) QUICK PICKLE

- 1 JALAPEÑO PEPPER, DESEEDED AND FINELY CHOPPED
- 4 BABY CUCUMBERS, SLICED
- 200 G CHERRY TOMATOES, QUARTERED
- ½ CUP APPLE CIDER VINEGAR OR WHITE WINE VINEGAR
- ½ RED ONION, PEELED AND THINLY SLICED
- PINCH OF SUGAR AND SALT

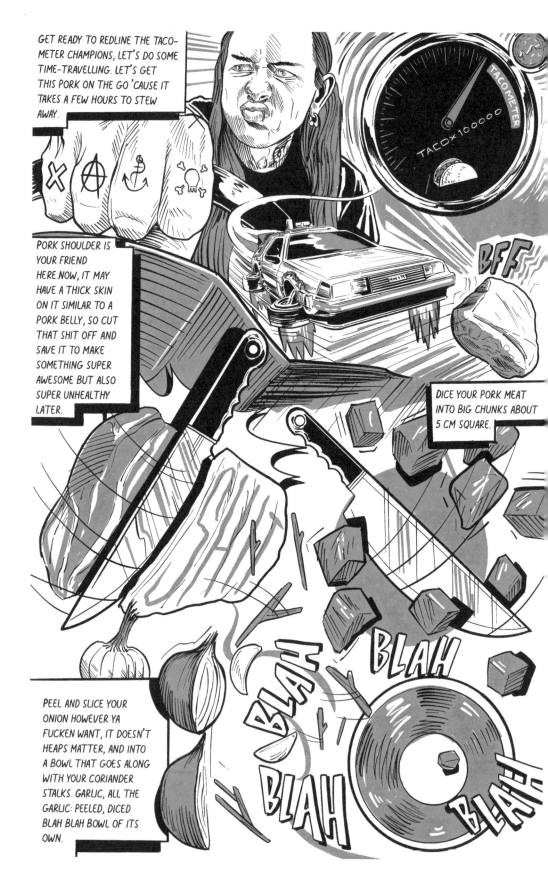

'IF YOU WANNA EAT GARBAGE, GO STICK YOUR HEAD IN A BIN.'

Pizza
Party

Who the bloody hell doesn't love pizza?
A crowd-pleaser if there ever was one.
Then there is the old frozen pizza wrapped
in plastic with all the shit on it that has slid
to one side and cooks into a disappointing hot
cardboard UFO that tastes about as good as
the box it came in. Making your own pizza
dough is pretty fucken easy and so fucken cool,
and you can extend the recipe to suit a shitload
of legends at once. Definitely a big feeling of joy
when you manage the whole event yourself.

MAKES: 2
COOKING TIME: about an hour
HECTOMETER: 6/10

INGREDIENTS

DOUGH

300 G TIPO '00' FLOUR OR STRONG PLAIN FLOUR, PLUS EXTRA FOR DUSTING
3/4 CUP (180 ML) WARM WATER
BIG PINCH OF SEA SALT FLAKES
1 TEASPOON CASTER SUGAR
7 G SACHET DRIED YEAST
2 TABLESPOONS EXTRA VIRGIN OLIVE OIL
50 G SEMOLINA FLOUR OR POLENTA, TO DUST BENCH

PIZZA SAUCE

2 TABLESPOONS EXTRA VIRGIN
  OLIVE OIL
2 CLOVES GARLIC
SMALL HANDFUL FRESH
  BASIL LEAVES
1 TABLESPOON TOMATO PASTE
400 G CAN GOOD-QUALITY
  PEELED TOMATOES
  (SAN MARZANO IF POSSIBLE)
1/2 TEASPOON BROWN SUGAR
PINCH O' SALT

TOPPING

150 G MOZZARELLA (THE HARD
  STUFF, OR EVEN GRATED)
2 BALLS BUFFALO MOZZARELLA,
  TORN
150 G PROSCIUTTO
FRESH BASIL LEAVES
HANDFUL OF BABY ROCKET
SHAVE OF PARMESAN CHEESE,
  IF YOU LIKE
CHILLI FLAKES, OPTIONAL

(BUT ADD WHATEVER YOU LIKE,
IT'S YOUR BLOODY PIZZA, MATE)

WHEEL of FORTUNE.

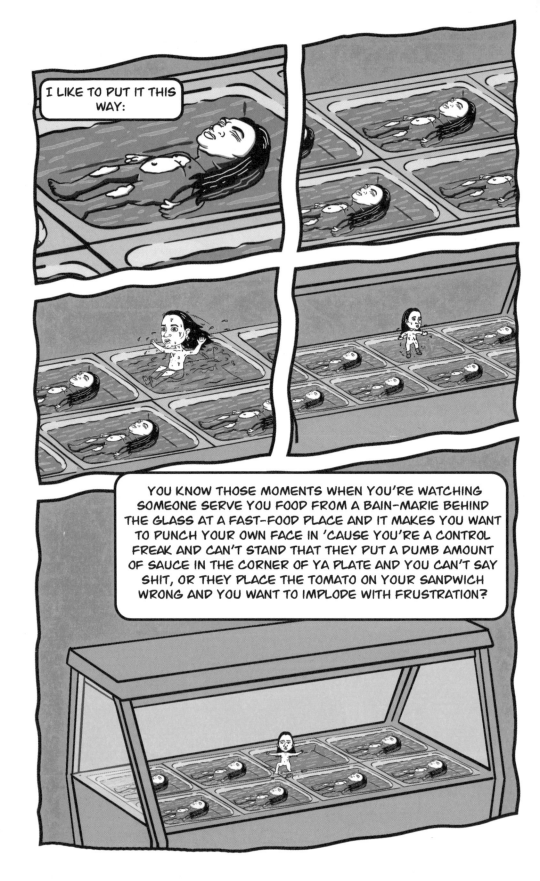

IS IT SHIT?

PINEAPPLE ON PIZZA

The timeless great debate, champions, about an ingredient that seems to cramp people's style in such a profound way that they feel the need to identify with it as some kind of personality trait. 'Oh, you like pineapple on your pizza? Well then, you're a massive dickhead,' seems to be the general sentiment on one side of the fence. A bit like the old coriander/cilantro chat: either you love it or you hate it, but I've never heard someone say they 'don't mind' eating it. It always has to be this extreme hard line in the sand that says you're either with us or against us. Obviously, I have a preference too, but before I get to it, let's break it down.

I suppose the most famous 'pineapple on a pizza' recipe has to be old mate the 'Hawaiian', whose origins are unsurprisingly not at all from Hawaii, let alone Naples, where the pizza was invented. In fact, it was invented in Canada by a fella called Sam.

Now, of course, the argument that pineapple's not a traditional pizza topping is, I suppose, a valid one, but my guess is that some of the very same people ordering shit like a 'godfather' or a fucken 'barbecue meat lovers' are quite possibly the very same pineapple haters. I'm not sure you're going to find a great deal of barbecue sauce at a traditional Napoli-style pizza joint, tough nuts.

Like my bolognese, I try to respect some aspects of cooking tradition as a nod to its roots, but pizza isn't a dish that is as rigid as bolognese sauce, it's a dish that has lots of different versions, so you're gonna end up with some loose units out there adding wild shit to it.

Nevertheless, I respect a good set of boundaries in one's life, and if pineapple not going on your pizza is one of them, then I can respect that. But as a flavour addition to a pizza . . .

No, I don't think it's shit. Soz about it.

PORK 'YEAH' BELLY

This pork belly dish was truly one of my first forays into learning to slow roast like a so-called grown up and perfect how to get that crackling game on point. It was one of the first big bangers in my roasting repertoire and is still one of my favourites. I think I must have cooked it every other day for months, roping in as many people as I could to come to my place to serve it to them. The rad thing about the belly cut of meat is that it's fairly inexpensive and when you're trying to be a fancy pants on the dole, it ticks a big lot of boxes in that regard. It does unfortunately lend itself to ticking a few weight-gain boxes too when you fucken eat it four nights a week like I did at one stage. I developed the habit of getting a little obsessed with cooking the same thing to perfection for a hot second. It's certainly not an everyday dish this one, but also . . . do what ya fucken want, eh?

SERVES: 4–6
COOKING TIME: just under 4 hours
HECTOMETER: 5/10

INGREDIENTS

- 1.5 KG PIECE BONELESS PORK BELLY
- 2 SMALL OR 1 LARGE ONION, PEELED AND SLICED INTO THICK RINGS
- 6–8 GARLIC CLOVES, PEELED AND BRUISED
- HANDFUL THYME LEAVES
- 1 TABLESPOON FENNEL SEEDS (ROUGHLY BUSTED APART IN A MORTAR AND PESTLE)
- OLIVE OIL
- SEA SALT FLAKES
- PEPPER
- 500 ML CHICKEN STOCK
- 250 ML BEER OR WHITE WINE
- 1 TABLESPOON PLAIN FLOUR

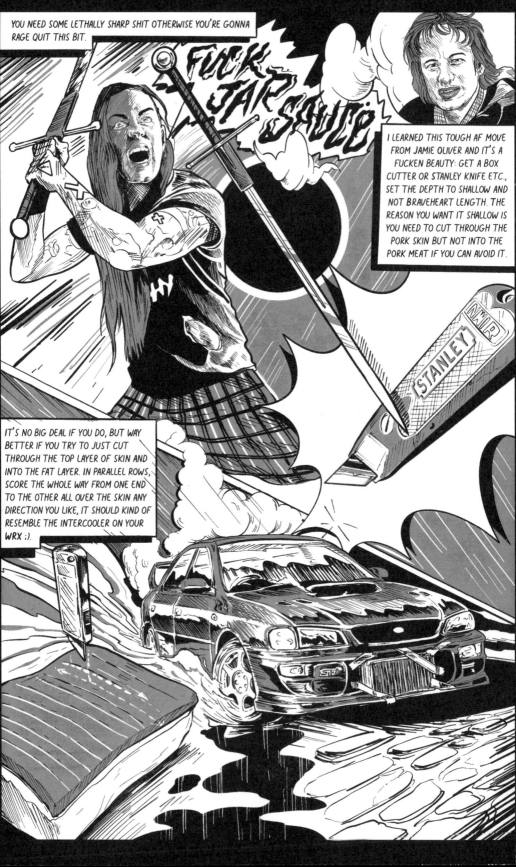

'LET'S NOT LET JAR SAUCES TURN US INTO UNINSPIRED DEADSHITS.'

RICE RICE
BABY

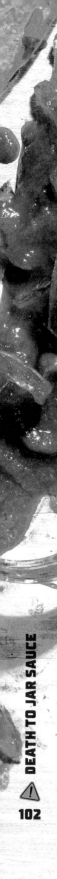

I have made a shitload of soggy bowls of over-soy-sauced trash in my time, trying to get fried rice to land the way it should. It was a couple of small things that helped me make that dream come true. Firstly, last night's rice or cold, cooked rice was just the ticket that gave me the courage to fry another day. And secondly, a bit like a lot of great dishes, it doesn't need a huge number of additions to get it across the line. In fact, fewer ingredients makes it go way harder . . . ease up on the soy sauce, turbo.

SERVES: 4

COOKING TIME: 10–15 mins (with pre-cooked rice)

HECTOMETER: 2.5/10

INGREDIENTS

4 CUPS COOKED WHITE RICE (COLD)
SHITLOAD OF GARLIC (6+ CLOVES), PEELED
I CARROT, PEELED
2 RED CHILLIES
4 FRENCH SHALLOTS (MORE EXPENSIVE, ANNOYING ONION), PEELED
250 G SPECK, BACON OR HAM (THE SAME WEIGHT OF GREEN BEANS, CAPSICUM AND CORN ARE RIPPER REPLACEMENTS FOR THE MEAT, IF YOU'RE VEGO)
2 EGGS
I CUP PEAS
VEG OR PEANUT OIL
2 TABLESPOONS OYSTER SAUCE (SUBSTITUTE MUSHROOM SAUCE OR EXCLUDE FOR VEG)
I-2 TABLESPOONS SOY SAUCE
3 SPRING ONIONS
SESAME OIL, TO SERVE (OPTIONAL)
CORIANDER AKA SOAP-TASTING POISON (OPTIONAL)

WHILE THE RICE IS COOLING,

CUT UP THE GARLIC,

CARROT,

CHILLI,

SHALLOTS

AND SPECK OR OTHER VEGGIES

INTO MODERATELY SMALL SIZES THAT GIVE OFF A 'COOKS FAST' VIBE AND BUNG IT ALL IN A BOWL.

CRACK YOUR EGGS INTO A BOWL

AND WHISK TOGETHER.

NOW, OVER TO THE STOVE AND GET YOURSELF A SMALL PAN.

CHUCK IT ON MEDIUM-LOW AND BUNG IN SOME OIL

(WHEN I USED SESAME OIL HERE,

UNCLE ROGER TOLD ME OFF ON YOUTUBE AS IT SHOULDN'T REALLY BE HEATED UP,

SO USE VEG OR PEANUT OIL, IF YOU'D PREFER).

DON'T ASK THE INTERNET TO REMIND YOU TO BUY A WOK

I learned a valuable lesson recently: never ask millions of people at once to remind you to buy a wok. I sometimes forget that a lot of what I do is on a platform that welcomes people's comments, so when I made my fried rice dish on screen and asked viewers to remind me after I'd forgotten to buy a new wok beforehand, I got what I asked for in spades. I still get emails about it more than a year later.

My recipe was a real hit on the channel, so much so that it was reviewed by several experts across the world, including Uncle Roger, who is a character that at the time made a lot of reaction/review videos about people's egg fried rice recipes. The character is fucken hilarious and played by a fella called Nigel Ng from the UK. (Side note: I actually have an uncle named Rodger in real life.) Nigel reached out and mentioned that Uncle Roger was gonna give my video a review, to which I replied something along the lines of, 'Big fan, mate. Hell yeah, go for it.' I'm not gonna lie, after seeing some of his other videos – particularly his one destroying Jamie Oliver's fried rice recipe – I was bracing myself for a fucking brutal serving. To my surprise, I came off pretty unscathed and was even complimented on my accuracy with most of it. So there you go, eh? I have since taken on board some of his advice on sesame oil usage, and it works a treat: just add it at the end, you beauty. As for his suggestion that I add MSG, I haven't gone there yet; I think the oyster sauce I use has a little in it, so might have already quietly ticked that box.

It's awesome how cooking something as simple as egg fried rice has brought me such amazing engagement with legends out there. I have the added bonus of learning a few things from not only you guys, but also mates and pro chefs alike. Most important lesson, though: don't ask the entire internet to remind you to buy a wok.

LAMB
MOUSSAKA
THERAPY

Just imagine a dish as therapeutic to eat as a lasagne, but instead of beef it's made with lamb and has layers of potato and eggplant as the pasta sheets . . . Imagine no more, champions! Moussaka is such a fucken rock 'n' roll dish, there are some incredible variations of it across the globe. Mine is based on the more traditional Greek style, as the combination of bechamel sauce and lamb mince suits me down to the bloody ground. The lamb and spice mix power combo will blow your bloody mind, and it'll no doubt be making a frequent appearance in your repertoire in no time. Get down and get with it, champions – it's worth every bit of effort, I swear.

SERVES: 6–8
COOKING TIME: a few hours
HECTOMETER: 7/10

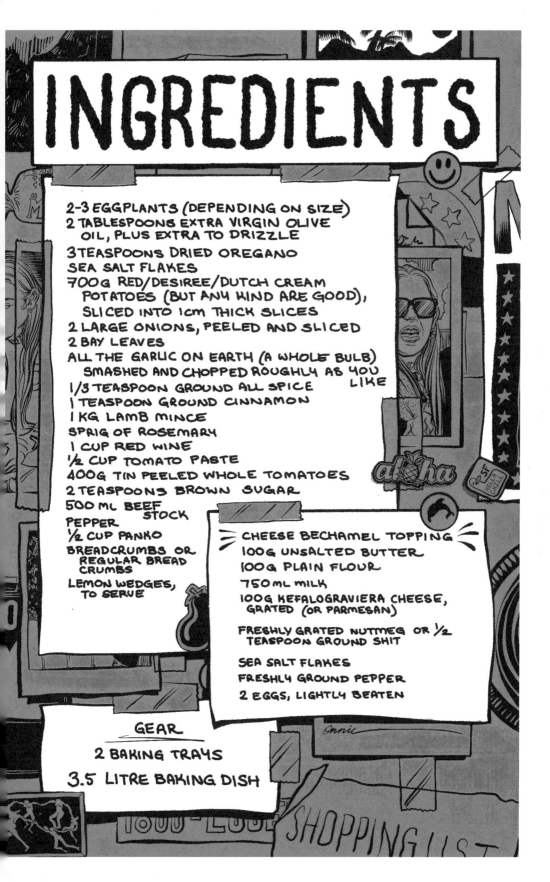

INGREDIENTS

2-3 EGGPLANTS (DEPENDING ON SIZE)
2 TABLESPOONS EXTRA VIRGIN OLIVE OIL, PLUS EXTRA TO DRIZZLE
3 TEASPOONS DRIED OREGANO
SEA SALT FLAKES
700G RED/DESIREE/DUTCH CREAM POTATOES (BUT ANY KIND ARE GOOD), SLICED INTO 1CM THICK SLICES
2 LARGE ONIONS, PEELED AND SLICED
2 BAY LEAVES
ALL THE GARLIC ON EARTH (A WHOLE BULB) SMASHED AND CHOPPED ROUGHLY AS YOU LIKE
1/3 TEASPOON GROUND ALL SPICE
1 TEASPOON GROUND CINNAMON
1 KG LAMB MINCE
SPRIG OF ROSEMARY
1 CUP RED WINE
½ CUP TOMATO PASTE
400G TIN PEELED WHOLE TOMATOES
2 TEASPOONS BROWN SUGAR
500 ML BEEF STOCK
PEPPER
½ CUP PANKO BREADCRUMBS OR REGULAR BREAD CRUMBS
LEMON WEDGES, TO SERVE

CHEESE BECHAMEL TOPPING

100G UNSALTED BUTTER
100G PLAIN FLOUR
750ML MILK
100G KEFALOGRAVIERA CHEESE, GRATED (OR PARMESAN)
FRESHLY GRATED NUTMEG OR ½ TEASPOON GROUND SHIT
SEA SALT FLAKES
FRESHLY GROUND PEPPER
2 EGGS, LIGHTLY BEATEN

GEAR

2 BAKING TRAYS
3.5 LITRE BAKING DISH

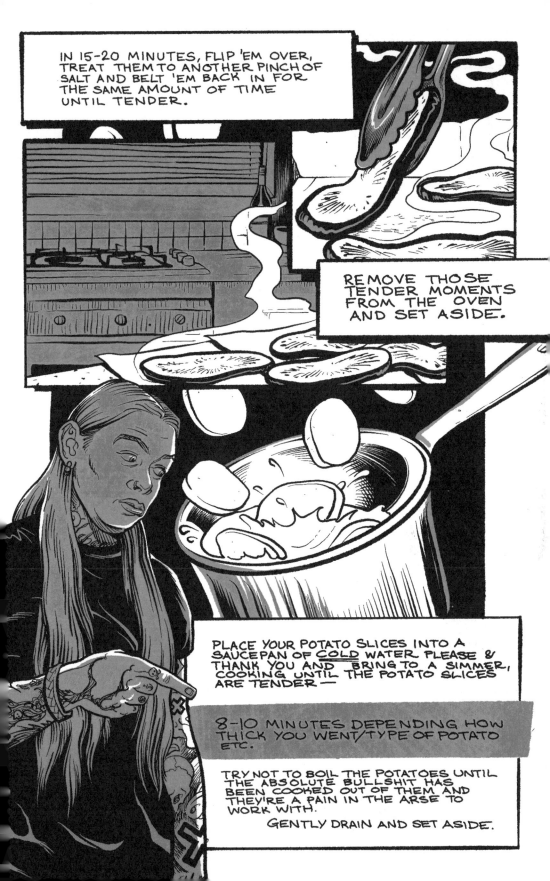

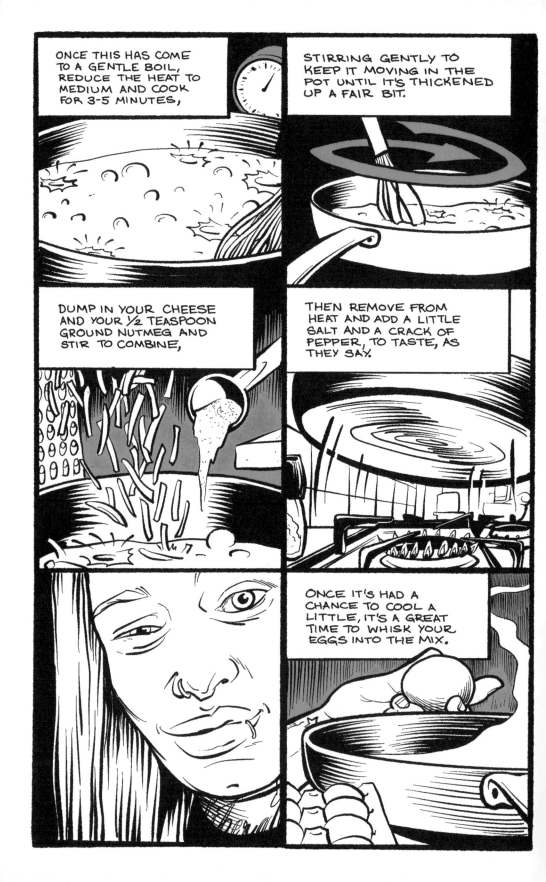

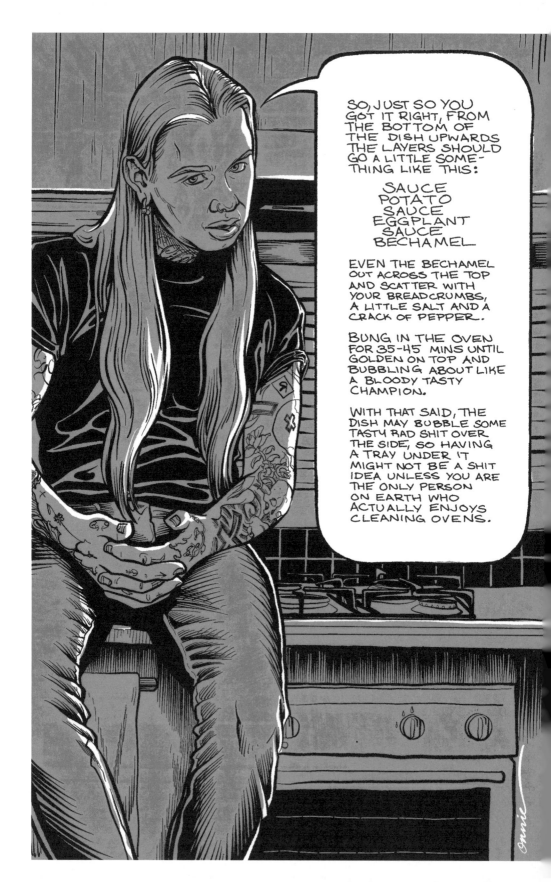

COGNITIVE
KITCHEN THERAPY

I have spent a lot of time in therapy in my life. It's a bloody good thing to have the opportunity to let rip about what's going on for you in a space that's dedicated to exactly that. Depressurising your fucken busy head is important, as is doing things that alleviate that shit for you. I find my noggin loves to look for trouble constantly, and if I don't give it something to do then I will likely find myself in deep shit. That's why putting together a good feed is so therapeutic, 'cause it can shut your shit-talking head up for a second, and lets you enjoy a bit of a breather.

Slower cooks are good for a bit of a well-focused rostered moment off. Take that last dish, for example; moussaka has a lot of parts to it and there is incidentally a lot of care and Lego-style building that goes into it. By the time you've put it all together and marvelled at your creation, let alone about how it tastes . . . you've accidentally kicked a mental health goal between several posts. The idea of doing something kind for someone else when you're not feeling too shit hot is actually a great way to shake off any heavy feelings and invite a different vibe to your otherwise tricky day. I find that cooking is the most red-hot way of doing exactly that. I love cooking for heaps of people, particularly when they are hungry or a bit skint. The joy of just seeing people so happy to experience something as simple as a meal is better than fucken eating it myself.

To be able to chip into a bit of joy in someone's day and leave your fucken nonsense behind for a hot second over a feed is champagne survival stuff – what a simple thing, but also such a profound moment, all at once. When I otherwise feel like a broken unit that can't even handle my day, I can shift gears and do something to help not only myself but other people too, and feel like everything is gonna be alright. It's nice not to feel so overwhelmed and useless on those days, as well as have a little flex of self-esteem.

HONEY BASTARD
CHICKEN

Honey mustard chicken is the most fucken relentlessly requested recipe on the channel and probably one of the most Defqon.1-level jar sauce abominations to ever hit the shelves. It's such rotten garbage that I went totally off that bastard of a sickly-sweet dish for years, but I'M BACK CHAMPIONS AND WE'VE FIXED IT!

The idea is to help you escape any chance of having to eat that trash again. I've loved a bit of sweet and savoury action all the way back to an unhealthy obsession with Lemon Crisp biscuits as a kid. I actually did an advert for Pizza Shapes when I was eleven years old and I got paid in Lemon Crisp biscuits . . . Dad ate half of them, I think. Anyway, I'm getting a little off track here – this isn't a freaken recipe for biscuits, but it is one for sweet and savoury chicken radness.

SERVES: 4–6
COOKING TIME: under an hour
HECTOMETER: 5/10

INGREDIENTS
8 MEDIUM OR 6 LARGE SKIN-ON BONELESS CHICKEN THIGHS
SALT
1 TABLESPOON VEGETABLE OIL
25 G UNSALTED BUTTER
1 ONION, PEELED AND SLICED
1 SMALL BUNCH PARSLEY, STALKS AND LEAVES CHOPPED,
BUT KEPT SEPARATE
6 GARLIC CLOVES, PEELED AND CHOPPED
1 TABLESPOON THYME LEAVES, CHOPPED
2 TABLESPOONS DIJON MUSTARD
2 TABLESPOONS WHOLEGRAIN MUSTARD
1½ TABLESPOONS HONEY
½ CUP WHITE WINE
1 CUP CHICKEN STOCK OR WATER
3 TEASPOONS PLAIN FLOUR
125 G CRÈME FRAÎCHE OR SOUR CREAM
(FULL-FAT STUFF WORKS BEST)

NOW YOU CAN OF COURSE DO THIS WITH CHICKEN BREAST BUT SINCE MAKING THE SHIFT TO CHICKEN THIGH, LIFE IN GENERAL HAS BECOME WAY BETTER. CHICKEN BREAST IS FINE AND ALL, BUT TAKES SOME WORK TO STOP IT FROM TASTING DRY AS A MOUTHFUL OF FUCKEN CHALK. SO LET'S CRACK ON WITH THE SKIN-ON THIGHS. SEASON THEM WITH SALT AND PLACE SKIN-SIDE DOWN INTO A ... WAIT FOR IT... COLD PAN! SOZ *WOT?* YEAH THAT'S RIGHT CHAMPION, A COLD PAN WITH A TABLESPOON OF OIL IN IT.

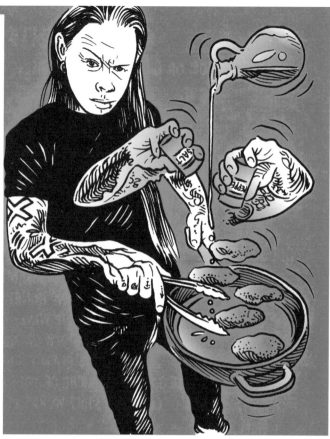

TURN ON THE STOVE TO A MEDIUM HEAT BUT **DON'T TOUCH** THE THIGHS.

WE WANT THEM TO STAY PUT FACE DOWN RENDERING IN THE OIL SO THEY GET SUPER CRISPY PANTS. KEEP THE HEAT AT MEDIUM UNTIL YOU HEAR IT STARTING TO SIZZLE ME TIMBERS, AND FROM THAT POINT IT'S 8 MINUTES UNTIL FLIP TIME.

ONCE THE SKIN SIDE IS GOLDEN BROWN TOWN, USE TONGS TO FLIP THEM OVER AND GIVE IT A HARD 5 ON THE OTHER SIDE (AT THE SAME HEAT).

IN A BOWL BUNG IN YOUR FLOUR AND SPOON IN A LITTLE OF THE PAN JUICE THEN WHISK TOGETHER INTO A PASTE-LIKE CONSISTENCY. NOW BACK INTO THE PAN WITH YOUR MAGICAL CHICKEN FLOUR PASTE ALONG WITH THE CRÈME FRAÎCHE OR SOUR CREAM AND COOK FOR A FEW MINUTES.

CRÈME FRAÎCHE

OMG WHAT THE FUCK IS THIS CHICKEN STILL DOING ON A FUCKEN PLATE RIGHT NOW? ALL GOOD, LET'S FIX THAT WAGON AND BUNG IT BACK IN TO THE MUSTARDY CREAMY NON JAR-EY GOODNESS WITH THE CHICKEN SKIN FACING UP SO THE SAUCE DOESN'T KILL ALL THAT CRISPY HARD WORK. GIVE IT AROUND 5 MINUTES IN THE SAUCE THERE BOSS; WE WANNA HEAT IT UP GOOD.

UNDERCOOKED CHICKEN IS A NOT-SO-FUN RIDE ON A SLIPPERY SLIDE TO BAD NEWS, SO MAKE SURE IT'S HEATED THROUGH.

I (DON'T) FEEL LIKE POULTRY THIS EVENING

I t's no secret that I take issue with shit jar sauce. The thing that frightens me more than the ingredients half the time is the fucken colour of it. Bechamel sauce in a jar has to be one of the most fascinatingly fucked up things I've ever laid my eyes on – it will forever look to me like a jar filled with clag glue and skim milk. All of these instant meals in a glass jar look pretty messed up to me, and the fact that they are called 'simmer sauce' just makes me laugh – what does that even mean? Oh, it's simmer flavoured, is it? One of my favourite horror shows is 'country French white wine'. I could write a whole book on my opinions on that flavour profile.

It's been a real target of mine to recreate these jars of gluggy blob in the kitchen and post them on my page – in fact it's very likely why you're reading this book. I often ask people what they wanna see me try next, and there are some ripper suggestions. I am eternally grateful for your amazing input there, champions.

I've gone through some real classic hits jar frighteners, such as stroganoff, carbonara and of course the infamous bolognese. Previously, I have never been tempted to recreate the honey mustard sauce from the brand whose name is a version of 'poultry this evening', even though it's been one of the most requested. I haven't historically been the biggest fan of the marriage of honey and mustard, but that's likely from having such intense memories of eating jarred versions of it. So I struggled to bring myself to attempt to repair the damage . . . nevertheless I put on my helmet and elbow pads and got in there to fix the problem.

There's always a way out of the jar, always.

THE
(CHICKEN)
WINGS OF LOVE

Let's not kid ourselves here, wings are
clearly the best part of the chicken.
But something magical happens when
you go and make them so much more
awesome by covering them in rad stuff and
deep frying them to a point where you're
almost concerned with how many of these
fucken things you could probably put away
in one sitting. This dish also gives us a
chance to make chipotle mayo together,
which is very trendy indeed and also super
fucken tasty. So drop kick that zinger
and let's make a winner.

SERVES: 4–6
COOKING TIME: 1.5 hours, including marinating
HECTOMETER: 6/10

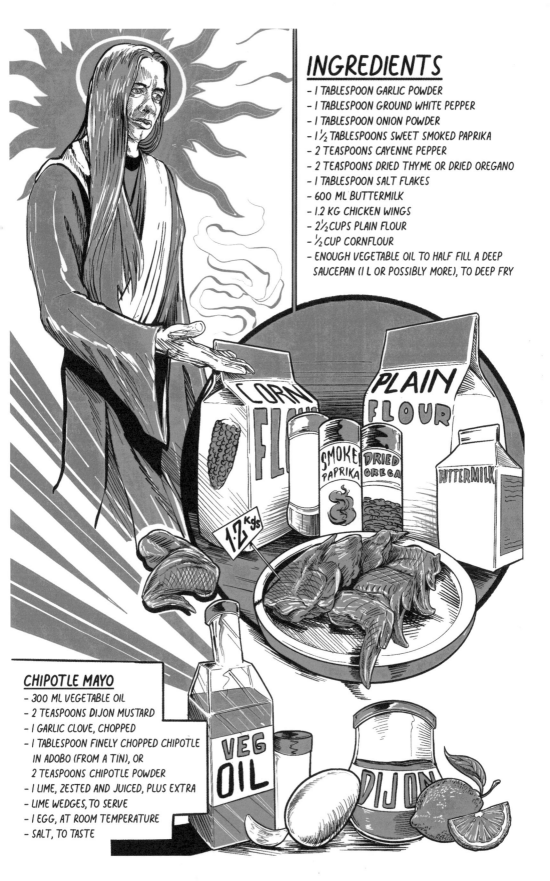

INGREDIENTS

- 1 TABLESPOON GARLIC POWDER
- 1 TABLESPOON GROUND WHITE PEPPER
- 1 TABLESPOON ONION POWDER
- 1½ TABLESPOONS SWEET SMOKED PAPRIKA
- 2 TEASPOONS CAYENNE PEPPER
- 2 TEASPOONS DRIED THYME OR DRIED OREGANO
- 1 TABLESPOON SALT FLAKES
- 600 ML BUTTERMILK
- 1.2 KG CHICKEN WINGS
- 2½ CUPS PLAIN FLOUR
- ½ CUP CORNFLOUR
- ENOUGH VEGETABLE OIL TO HALF FILL A DEEP
  SAUCEPAN (1 L OR POSSIBLY MORE), TO DEEP FRY

CHIPOTLE MAYO

- 300 ML VEGETABLE OIL
- 2 TEASPOONS DIJON MUSTARD
- 1 GARLIC CLOVE, CHOPPED
- 1 TABLESPOON FINELY CHOPPED CHIPOTLE
  IN ADOBO (FROM A TIN), OR
  2 TEASPOONS CHIPOTLE POWDER
- 1 LIME, ZESTED AND JUICED, PLUS EXTRA
- LIME WEDGES, TO SERVE
- 1 EGG, AT ROOM TEMPERATURE
- SALT, TO TASTE

'SOMETIMES YA JUST GOTTA THROW CAUTION TO THE RANGE HOOD AND TRY SOMETHING NEW.'

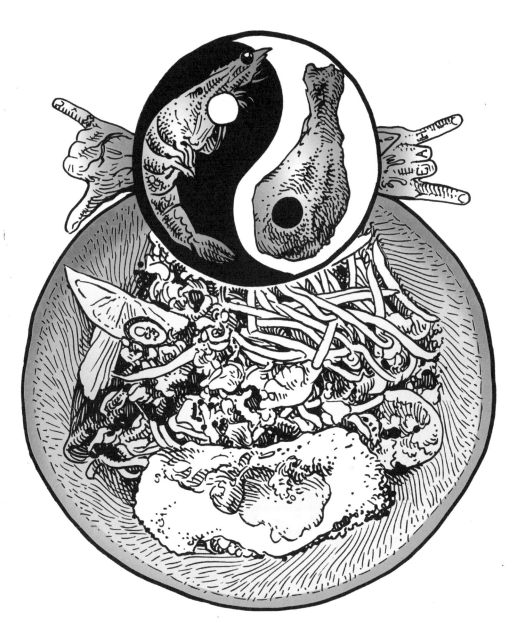

SURF AND TURF
MIE GORENG

NAT'S WHAT I RECKON

There's not a person I know who hasn't smashed the absolute shit out of a metric fuck-tonne of mie goreng packets in their time. Whether I've been dragging the bottom of the drawer for change to sort a feed, coming home hungry and late drunk af, or even just being up for a trusty, spicy, instant noodle kick in the arse, instant mie goreng has been there for my younger self in times when I've been stuck in a real jam. This might sound a touch contradictory to my whole 'fuck packet food' rhetoric, but I gotta pay tribute to this absolute institution of an instant meal and cook one that will hopefully make you shit yourself with excitement, and not because you regretted eating the third packet of instant ones for dinner three nights in a row.

SERVES: 4
COOKING TIME: 30 mins–1 hour
HECTOMETER: 5/10

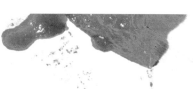

INGREDIENTS

250 G SHELLED AND CLEANED RAW PRAWNS
(FROM ABOUT 500 G SHELL-ON PRAWNS)
500 G BONELESS CHICKEN THIGH FILLETS
4 SPRING ONIONS
6 GARLIC CLOVES, PEELED AND FINELY CHOPPED
2 TABLESPOONS VEGETABLE OIL
1½ CUPS THINLY SLICED WHITE CABBAGE
1½-2 TABLESPOONS SAMBAL OELEK OR 2-3 TABLESPOONS SRIRACHA
1/3 CUP KECAP MANIS
JUICE OF 1 LIME PLUS 4 WEDGES, TO SERVE
1 TABLESPOON SOY SAUCE
1 TEASPOON SESAME OIL
400 G COOKED EGG NOODLES (LIKE HOKKIEN)
100 G BEAN SPROUTS
4 EGGS
CRISPY FRIED ONIONS AND THINLY SLICED RED CHILLI, TO SERVE

IF YOU BOUGHT PRAWNS STILL IN THEIR SHELLS— HOPEFULLY NICE ONES — THEN NOW IS A RIPPER TIME TO PEEL, CLEAN (SLICE DOWN THEIR BACK AFTER PEELING AND REMOVE THE POOP TUBE) AND SET THEM ASIDE.

DICE YOUR SKINLESS CHICKEN THIGHS INTO 2-CM WIDE STRIPS OR CHUNKS OR FUCKEN WHATEVER YA BLOODY WANT REALLY.

THINLY SLICE YOUR SPRING ONIONS, SETTING A PINCH ASIDE TO SERVE AT THE END. THE REST CAN GO IN A BOWL CHOPPED UP WITH YOUR GARLIC.

IF YOU HAVE A WOK, THIS IS A SICK BIT OF KIT FOR THIS GIG SO GRAB IT AND FANG IT ON THE STOVE, ADD THE OIL AND CRANK THE HEAT TO HIGH. (YOUR BIGGEST FRYING PAN IS THE NEXT BEST THING.)

AWAY WE GO IN WITH THE CHICKEN THIGHS TO STIR FRY FOR 4-5 MINUTES TILL BROWNED. WHAT DO YA KNOW, JACK, IT'S TIME TO ADD THAT SURF (PRAWNS) TO THE TURF (CHOOK) ALONG WITH THE SPRING ONIONS AND GARLIC. TOSS THIS LOT AROUND FOR A COUPLE OF MINUTES.

THE
BREAKFAST
CLUB

When I first left home aged seventeen (I think?), I was far from a culinary wiz. Jar sauce was on high rotation, as was smoking weed and other generally lazy activities like playing video games and not giving a huge shit about myself. I have a vivid recollection of eating a jar of stroganoff that I cooked with chuck beef in it . . . holy shit, is that a scary memory. Not only is chuck beef not something you should cook for a short amount of time, but when also paired with the jar of horrors it's a match made in hell. Along with meals like that were the fuck-tonnes of the infamous packets of instant noodles, and holy dooley, did I go through a few of those. Chuck a few bongs into the mix and you are shitting yourself like a laser pointer, so much so that you feel like you may need to start looking for the number of your local vicar in the Yellow Pages.

It was quite a gut-smashing journey, those early days of making myself food. I came to realise a few things as time went on, including that eating takeaway garbage actually becomes quite fucken expensive real fast, and that half the pre-made shit you buy at the shops tastes like total trash. Learning how to cook even a few things well made me excited to recreate and stick it to a lot of that other landfill I was driving into myself. I ended up discovering something I was pretty okay at, and I was also able to save me a shitload of money to buy other useless shit I didn't need.

The big breakthrough was when I discovered the pure joy that is share-house roasting. My flatmates and I would all chip in and go to the shops to buy these big cuts of meat, then come home to prepare them for the whole house. We would do this on repeat and feed a huge house full of hungry, partied-out legends. It was a fucken good time and helped me embrace my love of cooking for people, and often for lots of people. I spent a shitload of time studying how to cook the dishes that I wanted to try. I relentlessly watched 'how to nail the perfect roast' videos on YouTube and, to be honest, got so carried away that I think I ate a roast dinner every night for weeks on end.

I am grateful that I received such a warm reception from my mates when I would cook food, as it gave me the confidence to keep trying to perfect my dishes. I'm such a social butterfly of a person in general – I love my mates so much, and any excuse to have them around to hang out made me feel like things were gonna be okay. My head chews me up and spits me out every day, so having some company can be a nice chance to take a break from that shit.

I was on the dole for a long time due to my mental health problems so I had a bit of spare time on my hands most days. The first thing I would do in the morning was get up and think of what I could cook for everyone in my house that night, and who else I could invite around for dinner. I even had a breakfast club going for a minute there, where me and my mate Steve would put on these fucken extra af spreads for everyone in the mornings on the weekend. We would meticulously fascinate over the perfect poached eggs technique, or fry up a bullshit amount of eggs, mushrooms, bacon . . . the list of brekkie ingredients goes for days. Steve and I even rolled the dice making our own duck prosciutto which, let me tell you, does not feel safe at all. Fanging raw duck meat in a bunch of salt and herbs and leaving it out to hang and dry for a few weeks in the back of a truck seems like a great way to send yourself to the cemetery arse first. I'm pretty sure the little cheesecloth cocoons filled with salted duck just swung about in the back of Steve's truck that he was living in at the time as well as driving to work and back in every day. Well, what do you know? After weeks of this raw, salted duck breast hanging in the van, we sliced it up and bravely went for it: fucking amaaaaaaazing.

I went a bit mad for the whole cooking thing, really. I would almost demand that everyone come over and try my new 'thing' I was into. I loved it because it gave me this sense of being able to care for the people around me and express some real effort to show how important they all were to me. Food is nice like that, as it says a lot of things to a lot of people when you maybe don't know how to say them out loud. Eating food together was this bonding moment where we weren't all getting totally fucken hammered all the time, drowning our sorrows. Cooking and hanging out was such a huge escape from feeling like I was being swallowed up and spat out by the universe. I will be honest though, we did get pretty fucken bombed at a few of these cook ups.

Cooking a belter of a brekkie doesn't have to be this whole fucken palaver all the time. Simply working on getting your poached egg just right (fresh eggs, btw), and having that angelic thing on a slice of sourdough, has been enough to wow my tricky head into a victory for the morning. It set the pace for a more manageable day and didn't even take that long.

Some people might worry that cooking food is going to end up this super intimidating event because often it's made to look like it has to be 'just so' all the time. That's not to say you can't fucken nail a dish, but the road to cooking your signature thing may very well be paved with amazing flavour and some of the tastiest fuck-ups of all time. You don't have to twice cook things and dry them in vans for weeks for it to be a killer feed; a dish with only three fucken ingredients in it can easily get you on the front cover of the *I don't even suck at cooking* gazette.

Such a great way to go on an adventure when you're not up for the literal hike. And an awesome move to tell someone that you're thinking of them when they need a mate.

As for jar sauce, it's a great way to tell someone to go fuck themselves without needing to use your words too, haha.

FISH CAKES

Just imagine it was everyone's birthday every day and you didn't have to go to work or school or deal with any fuckwits 'cause you're a fish as well, which is weird, but also cool 'cause you're also eternally at a pool party in the ocean . . . (*takes deep breath*) aaaaaand someone's made you a cake and you also made them a cake and they are both made out of fish, which again sounds weird at first, BUT fish sometimes eat other types of fish too, which is totally chill when you're a fish at a birthday party, and plus we are making your favourite kind of fish cake so whoo hooooooooooo!

SERVES: 3–4
COOKING TIME: about 1 hour*
HECTOMETER: 3–6/10*

* depending on whether you make your own curry paste
and how staunch your blender/food processor is

INGREDIENTS

500 G SKINLESS WHITE FISH FILLETS (LIKE BASA, LING OR
    BLUE-EYE TREVALLA), CHOPPED UP HEAPS AS
½ BUNCH CORIANDER (STALKS AND LEAVES),
    ROUGHLY CHOPPED
3 MAKRUT/LIME LEAVES, THINLY SLICED
2 TABLESPOONS FISH SAUCE
2 TEASPOONS BROWN SUGAR
2-3 TABLESPOONS RED CURRY PASTE (SEE SOUP RECIPE
    TO MAKE YOUR OWN)
PINCH O' SALT
1 EGG
¼ CUP RICE FLOUR
2 TABLESPOONS FINELY GRATED GINGER
75 G GREEN BEANS
2 TABLESPOONS VEGETABLE OIL

CHILLI OR SWEET CHILLI SAUCE, EXTRA CORIANDER LEAVES
    AND LIME WEDGES, TO SERVE

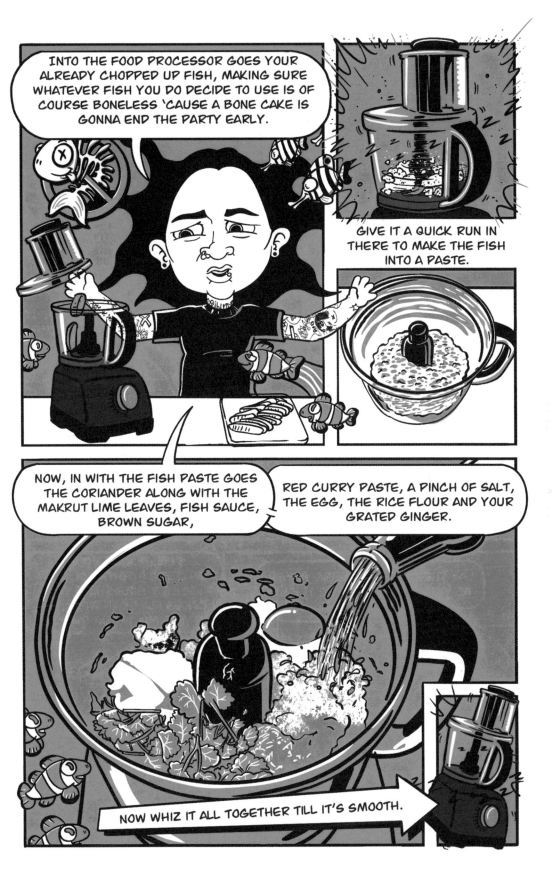

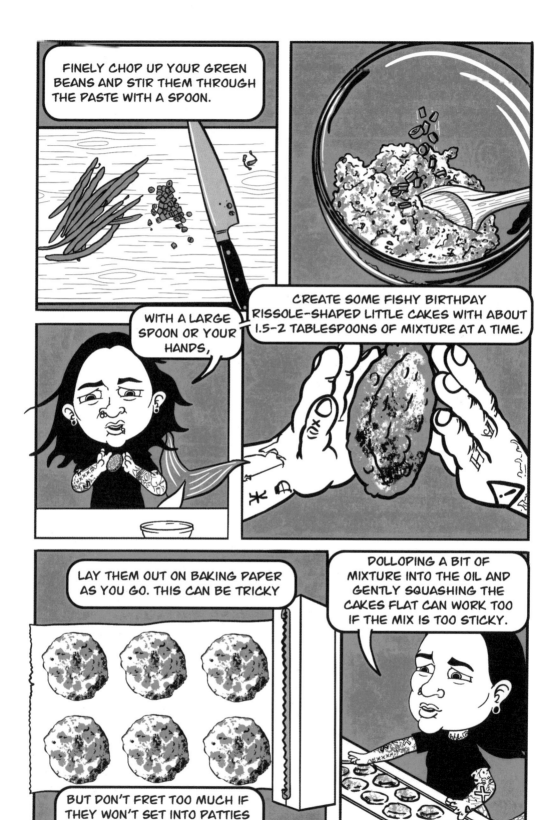

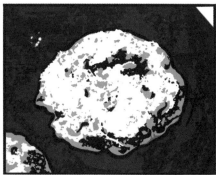

ONTO SOME PAPER TOWEL THEY GO FROM THE PAN.

GRAB YOUR CHILLI/SWEET CHILLI SAUCE, SOME CORIANDER LEAVES, SOME LIME WEDGES

AND A PARTY WHISTLE 'CAUSE IT'S TIME TO PARTY FISH CAKE STYLE.

IS IT SHIT?

BIRTHDAY PARTIES

We all love an excuse for a party, and a birthday is a tried and true reason to guilt everyone into rocking up to some annoying bar or mini golf thing that they wouldn't otherwise go to. Turning another year older is great when you're a kid because it often represents scoring free shit, being closer to not being told what to do so much and therefore having more freedom and money to buy more stupid shit.

As an adult over 21 years old, I find celebrating the encore of getting older to be something that's less and less necessary to carry on about. Don't get me wrong, I love an excuse to get together with people and will very occasionally pull the birthday card (punny bday joke for you there) to make it happen, but objectively I think making a big song and dance about being born every year doesn't need to keep happening, does it? I mean, at a distance, making people do stuff with you because you're older now is strange to me. And let's not forget all this pressure to gift people stupid shit that you're unsure whether or not they'll even like. Plus if you can't afford to buy them said trash, you feel guilty, and don't even mention regifting accidents (as seen on page 2). If you forget someone's birthday, then goddamn, you demon, for not remembering when they were born, along with every other person you know. If it wasn't for Facebook most of us would have no idea when people's birthdays were these days, anyway.

I've always been a bit anti all the normal stuff in life, so it makes sense that I am taking aim at birthday parties. I suppose all I'm trying to say is that often people don't need anyone's permission to get loose. It doesn't have to be for this big reason like your age. Congratulations for being older and all, but to me it seems a little morbid that we are all so fascinated with celebrating it repeatedly. You're not dead yet, bravo!

Yeah, kinda shit.

One of the most beautiful things in life is the simplicity of friendship. Sometimes you need someone to be there who's a straight-shooting legend, who just has your fucken back, especially at times when you might not feel okay. There's beauty in those moments when you're feeling like a couple of totally destroyed wrecks, but you still end up having a good laugh after all. This ceviche recipe is inspired by one such moment, when my two best mates and I formed a mighty trio of untouchable togetherness!

We set a goal to have a fucken shit-hot pool party up north, eat some good food and get through the tough times together. Ceviche is something that cemented the memory of that time together for me – I remember us all being amazed at how such a simple dish worked such fucken magic and took some of the worry away for just a moment. Times are tough, maybe we all just need to have ceviche on the beach, eh?

SERVES: 2–3
COOKING TIME: less than 30 mins
HECTOMETER: 2/10

INGREDIENTS

- 500g RAW KINGFISH, SNAPPER or BARRAMUNDI FILLETS, skin off and ↳ Pinboned

- JUICE OF 3 LIMES

- ZEST OF 1 LIME

- 1-2 JALAPEÑOS finely chopped (OR 2 REGULAR LONG CHILLIES)

- 1 GARLIC CLOVE, peeled and ↳ minced

- SALT AND PEPPER

- 1 TEASPOON TABASCO ↳ plus extra to taste

- 2 TABLESPOONS GOOD-QUALITY OLIVE OIL

- 4 BABY LEBANESE CUCUMBERS, thinly sliced

- 250G CHERRY TOMATOES, halved

- ½ BUNCH CORIANDER, stalks and leaves, washed and chopped

- A SPRING ONION OR 2 SHALLOTS, thinly sliced

- 1 LARGE AVOCADO cut into 2cm pieces

- CORN CHIPS

- A GOOD MATE TO SHARE A COLD ONE WITH!

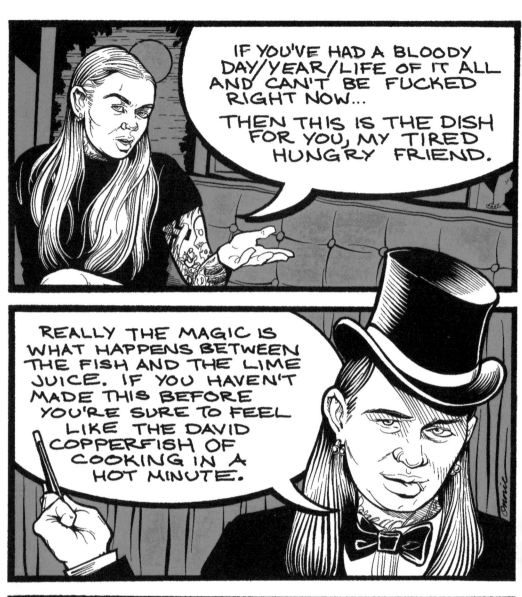

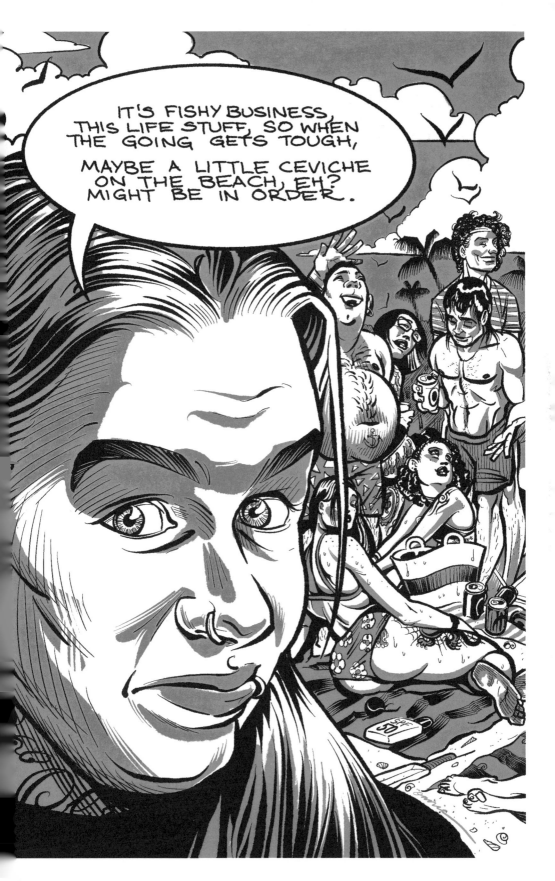

THE SHARE HOUSE VEGGIE BOX PALAVER

I am a big fan of saving your bucks and all chipping in as a team to get a good, affordable feed going, but there are some things I have tried to do as a group that haven't quite worked out. The veggie box collective is one of them.

I used to be a part of a veggie box collective, which for those of you playing at home is a scheme where a bunch of share houses – let's say five different ones – pool together a bunch of money each week in an effort to buy vegetables in bulk and divide them among the housemates. Each week one house does the shopping and divides and delivers it to the others in the collective. Great idea at a distance, as it only costs five bucks on average a week per person, and between that many houses you have enough money to go to the markets and buy a fucking shitload of food in bulk for cheap – cool, great . . .

The problem with this utopia is that you're talking about typically around twenty people with all sorts of 'favourite veggies' they like, so when it comes to that house's week to go rage the markets and they happen to have an unhealthy fucken love for squash or zucchini, you end up with a fat box filled full of fucken zucchini and squash and then people have to make stupid shit with dickhead amounts of zucchini in it all week. Share house group feeds already have a high rotation curry issue as far as I'm concerned, and buying shit like seventeen zucchini doesn't help. Don't get me wrong here, champion, I love a zucchini, I have a fucken fritter recipe in here for fuck's sake, but let's cut the shit and agree that 236 zucchini a week is at least 200 too many.

Some weeks it would be our turn to go to the markets, but because we were all hungover ghouls and not over-achieving, early-rising carrot juicers, we got reprimanded and eventually kicked out for delivering our boxes too late. I, of course, wanted to put heaps of stupid shit in the box to try and make people laugh when it was our turn, but I don't think that went well, either. I had my heart set on pumping it full of lollies and random cheap shit from the markets as a joke . . . but there will be none of that, this is a very serious box that needs to be taken very, very seriously.

'SHARE HOUSE GROUP FEEDS ALREADY HAVE A HIGH ROTATION CURRY ISSUE AS FAR AS I'M CONCERNED.'

I think if you're going to have a random vegetable collective then you need to chill out on the zucchini, or just start a fucken sick zucchini group, or maybe find a smaller number of houses to do it with. I mean, maybe develop a fucken sense of humour about it, they are fucken vegetables, for fuck's sake . . . relax, zucchini pants.

'DON'T BE A
GRUB AND COOK
SHIT OUT OF
A PACKET.
FUCKEN MAKE
IT YOURSELF.'

RED CURRY SWEET POTATO SOUP

I reckon sweet potato and red curry
are two good mates just waiting to hang out.
Imagine you were eating an amazingly silky,
sweet but savoury soup that was also
kind of a Thai curry flavour . . .
Sounds wild, is rad. Let's do it!

SERVES: 3–4
COOKING TIME: about 1 hour*
HECTOMETER: 6.5/10*

* if you make the curry paste

CURRY PASTE
INGREDIENTS

- 6 DRIED CHILLIES, SOAKED IN HOT WATER FOR 20 MINUTES, DRAINED
- 1 TEASPOON CUMIN SEEDS
- 1 TEASPOON CORIANDER SEEDS
- 1 TEASPOON BLACK PEPPERCORNS
- ROOTS FROM 1 BUNCH CORIANDER, WASHED (RESERVE STALKS AND LEAVES FOR SOUP)
- 1 TABLESPOON MINCED GALANGAL (OR GINGER)
- 4 FRESH LONG RED CHILLIES, PLUS EXTRA SLICES, TO SERVE
- 1 STALK LEMONGRASS, WHITE AND TENDER PART ONLY, ROUGHLY CHOPPED
- 2 MAKRUT LIME LEAVES
- 4 GARLIC CLOVES, PEELED
- 1½ TEASPOONS SHRIMP PASTE (OR 1 TABLESPOON FISH SAUCE)
- 2 SMALL RED ESCHALLOTS, PEELED AND ROUGHLY CHOPPED

SOUP INGREDIENTS

- 1 ONION
- A WHOLE BULB OF GARLIC
- 1 LEEK
- 800 G SWEET POTATO, PEELED AND CUT INTO 3CM PIECES
- 400 G BUTTERNUT PUMPKIN, PEELED AND CUT INTO 3CM PIECES
- 2 TABLESPOONS VEGETABLE OIL
- $\frac{1}{3}$-$\frac{1}{2}$ CUP RED CURRY PASTE
- 1 LITRE VEGETABLE OR CHICKEN STOCK
- 400 ML COCONUT MILK
- 1 LIME, JUICED
- CRISPY DRIED ONION TO SERVE

'IF A RECIPE
EVER SAYS TO
PUT TWO CLOVES
OF GARLIC IN
SOMETHING,
TELL IT TO FUCK OFF
AND STICK FIVE IN.
COS GARLIC'S THE BEST.
FUCK IT.'

VEGENATOR 2:
JUDGEMENT TRAY LASAGNE

NAT'S WHAT I RECKON

'My mission is to protect you' from shitty lasagne. The amazing stuff that can go into a veggie lasagne is fucken awesome – I occasionally prefer a good veg one over a meat version because of all the amazing layers of flavours you can get going on. This dish is layer upon layer of action-packed radness. So let's get terminating our hunger and prepare for Vegenator 2: Judgement Tray.

SERVES: 6–8
COOKING TIME: coupla hours
HECTOMETER: 6/10

INGREDIENTS

800 G - 1 KG BUTTERNUT PUMPKIN
2 TABLESPOONS OLIVE OIL
SALT
PEPPER
1 TEASPOON CHILLI FLAKES
2 TEASPOONS DRIED THYME
375-400G FRESH LASAGNE SHEETS, OR SOME PRE-COOKED
  UNFRESH ONES
300 G MOZZARELLA, COARSELY GRATED
100 G RICOTTA
50G FINELY GRATED PARMESAN

SAUCE

30 G BUTTER OR ¼ CUP EXTRA VIRGIN OLIVE OIL
3 CARROTS, PEELED AND DICED FINELY
2 ONIONS, PEELED AND CHOPPED
3 CELERY STICKS, DICED FINELY
1 MILLION GARLIC CLOVES, PEELED
  AND CHOPPED (JK, 6-8 CLOVES WILL DO)
2 BIRD'S EYE CHILLIES, CHOPPED (OPTIONAL)
SPRIG ROSEMARY
1 CUP RED WINE
1 X 400 G TIN BROWN LENTILS, DRAINED
2 X 400 G TINS WHOLE PEELED TOMATOES
2 TABLESPOONS TOMATO PASTE
1 TABLESPOON BROWN SUGAR
2 CUPS VEGETABLE OR CHICKEN STOCK

GEAR YA NEED

BAKING TRAY LINED
WITH BAKING PAPER

21 X 28 CM BAKING DISH

SPINACH RICOTTA LAYERNATOR

500 G RICOTTA (DELI BASKET RICOTTA -
  THE SHIT THAT COMES IN WATER IN A BASKET)
150 ML MILK
150 G FETA
2 BUNCHES (APPROX. 100 G) ENGLISH SPINACH
HANDFUL BASIL LEAVES

LAY ON A LINED BAKING TRAY
AND DRIZZLE WITH OLIVE OIL,
SCATTER WITH SALT, PEPPER, A PINCH OF CHILLI FLAKES
AND 1 TEASPOON DRIED THYME,
THEN BASH INTO THE OVEN FOR 25-30 MINUTES OR UNTIL TENDER-NATION CAN BE DETECTED.

COOK FOR 10-15ISH MINUTES UNTIL THEY ARE NICE AND SOFT.
FANG IN YOUR SPRIG OF ROSEMARY AND STIR THROUGH FOR ANOTHER MINUTE,
FOLLOWED BY YOUR RED WINE TO DEGLAZENATE THE PAN FOR 3 MINUTES.
34589 67865
56760 45389
09897 43544
34589 67865
56760 45389
09897 43544
34589 67865
56760 45389
09897 43544
DETECTING RED WINE

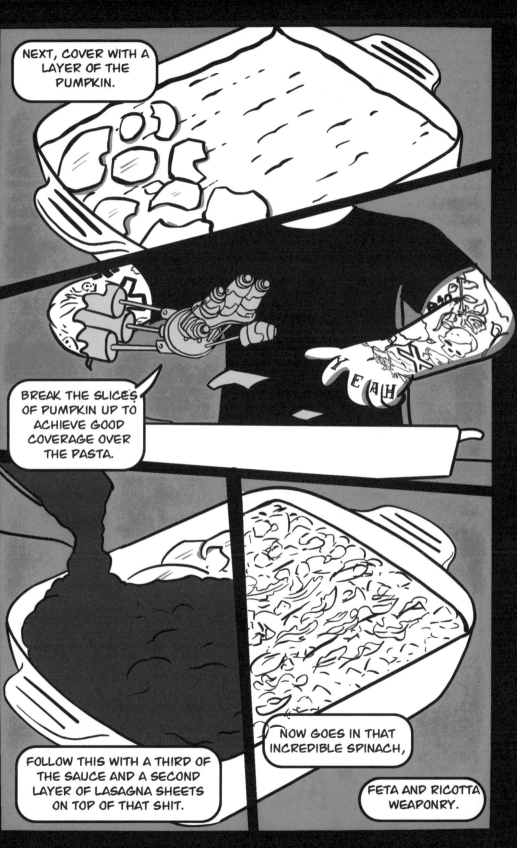

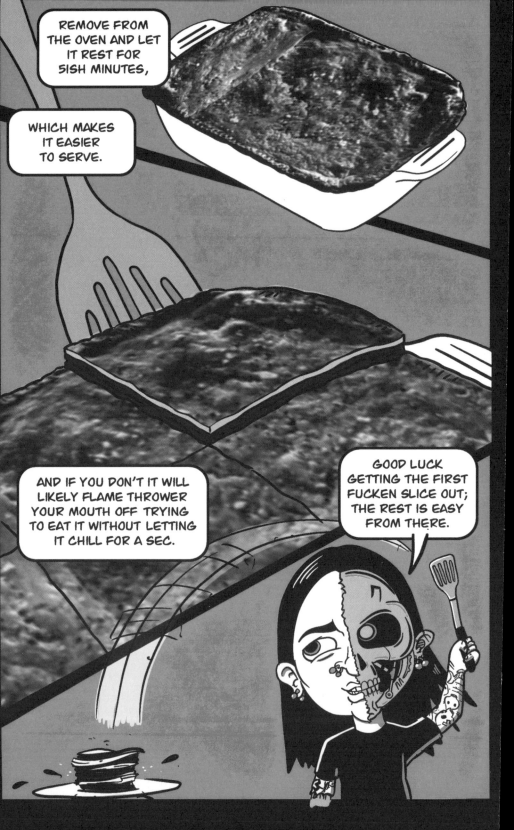

ACTION FILM PLOTS

Love a good lot of OTT action. Often the less realistic the plot is, the better.

I admire the verve of some movie franchises and their ability to not only find the funds to keep pumping out sequels, remakes and reboots, but also to flog a dead horse down to its fucking skeleton. If you have watched any of the many *Fast & Furious* movies, for example, you will know what I'm talking about. Like, how many of these fucken things are there in the world – forty-five? It truly takes franchise to a new level. From having a tug-of-war battle in the middle of the city and getting away with it, to driving a Mustang off a cliff and inexplicably catching a hook and swinging over to another cliff *and* landing safely with the car still running . . .? And where the fuck do they keep getting these cars from? Are they supposed to be undercover spies? I don't fully understand the premise of any of these movies or why the cars are so important to their 'missions'. PLUS driving around in a super fucken loud V8, constantly breaking all the speed limits and doing endless burnouts seems to just happen with no consequences? Love it.

Anything Steven Seagal has been in is a champagne example of action movies being a little extra. It seems like half the martial arts techniques are just made up on the spot, and the plots are so fucking off their head, it's wild. In one film he wakes up from a six-year coma and pushes himself out of a hospital in the bed to escape the bad guys, and within a week is back on his feet fighting people. If you were in a coma for any amount of time you certainly wouldn't be waking up and leaving the hospital on the same day, let alone punching on with bad guys just days later.

Road House is another belter of a movie that makes no real-world sense. Patrick Swayze just turns up and fights the entire bar to 'fix it', and eventually beats up enough people that the bar turns into an awful-looking RSL.

I think it's a bit like 'chewing gum for the brain' as my father would say. Sometimes you need a break in your head rather than an intellectual art-house journey. These films are so popular because they are so over the top and entertaining, their explosions and terrible scripts making you laugh and sometimes cry.

Plus the facts just ruin a good story.

Not shit, but totally shit.

'NOW THAT I APPRECIATE WHAT ACTUAL FOOD IS, I KNOW THAT EATING LIKE A MASSIVE FUCKWIT MAKES YOU FEEL LIKE SHIT.'

GNOCCH-ON OR FUCK OFF
CHILLI TOMATO GNOCCHI

NAT'S WHAT I RECKON

Harsh name I know, but here's the thing – one
of my best mates in the world and
I both have matching tattoos on our stomachs
that say 'Rock On Or Fuck Off',
so I kinda had to. This recipe is an overzealous
way of saying go hard or
go home, but with gnocchi in mind.
You can make gnocchi without potato
and just flour that's faster, but we
are rockin' the fuck on here, so let's
make my favourite type of gnocchi:
chilli tomato potato gnocchi.

SERVES: 3–4
COOKING TIME: a bit over 2 hours
HECTOMETER: 5/10

INGREDIENTS

GNOCCHI

1 KG SIMILAR SIZED SEBAGO POTATOES (THE DIRTY ONES)
125 G PLAIN FLOUR, PLUS EXTRA TO DUST
1 EGG, LIGHTLY BEATEN
SALT
SHAVED PARMESAN, TO SERVE
SMALL HANDFUL OF BASIL LEAVES, TO SERVE
PEPPER

CHILLI TOMATO SAUCE

1½ TABLESPOONS BUTTER
1 LARGE ONION, PEELED AND DICED
1 FUCKEN WHOLE BULB OF GARLIC (6-8 CLOVES), PEELED AND DICED
3 BIRD'S EYE CHILLIES, DESEEDED AND CHOPPED
2 × 400 G TINS OF CRUSHED OR WHOLE PEELED TOMATOES (SAN MARZANO RULES IF YOU CAN FIND IT)
1 TABLESPOON BROWN SUGAR
SALT
PEPPER

GEAR:
2 BAKING TRAYS
POTATO RICER (OPTIONAL)

WHILE THAT SHIT IS CHILLING OUT, LET'S MAKE THE SAUCE. INTO A SAUCEPAN OVER A MEDIUM-HIGH HEAT GOES YOUR BUTTER FOLLOWED BY YOUR ONIONS TO COOK OFF FOR 3-4 MINUTES UNTIL SOFTENED, THEN IN GOES YOUR GARLIC AND YOUR CHILLI FOR ANOTHER 1-2 MINUTES. NOW BY ALL MEANS FUCKEN BASH IN A SHITLOAD OF CHILLI IF YOU LOVE IT SICK, LIKE I DO.

MY SUGGESTION OF 3 CHILLIES IS ME BEING REASONABLE HERE BUT BY ALL MEANS, FUCKEN BELT MORE IN IF YOU'RE FEELING BRAVE.

NOW SEND IT WITH YOUR TOMATOES AND SUGAR, BRING TO A SIMMER AND DROP THE HEAT RIGHT DOWN WITH A LID ON AND COOK FOR 15-20 MINUTES.

WHILE THAT IS CARRYING ON OVER THERE, LET'S MAKE THE GNOCCHI, CHAMPION. GRAB TWO BAKING TRAYS AND COVER EACH WITH BAKING PAPER. THAT COOL, BACKWARDS-HAT-WEARING MASHED POTATO IS GONNA NEED THE FLOUR, EGG AND SALT FOLDED INTO IT. GET IN THERE AND MIX THE FUCKEN SHIT OUT OF IT. IF IT'S STILL WET AND UNMANAGEABLE, ADD MORE FLOUR AS NEEDED OR UNTIL YOU CAN GET IT OUT OF THE BOWL EASILY.

PLAIN WHITE
FLOUR

ON A LIGHTLY FLOURED SURFACE DUMP THAT POTATO BALL OUT AND WORK IT LIKE DOUGH, KNEAD IT LIKE YOU MEAN IT FOR AT LEAST 5 MINUTES SO IT'S ALL BLENDED TOGETHER, AGAIN ADDING A LITTLE FLOUR AS YOU GO IF IT'S STICKING TO THE BENCH.

NOW TURN IT ALL INTO A LUMP/BALL AND WITH A LIGHTLY FLOURED KNIFE (YES THERE IS FLOUR ON EVERYTHING BY NOW) CUT THE DOUGH INTO QUARTERS. ROLL ONE SECTION AT A TIME INTO A LONG SAUSAGE-LIKE SHAPE ABOUT 2.5 CM THICK ON A ... WAIT FOR IT ... FLOURED BENCH. RE-FLOUR THAT KNIFE AND CUT THE LOG INTO 3-CM SECTIONS AND PLACE ON THE PREPARED BAKING TRAY.

'NOT ALL DISHES WITH GREEN SHIT IN THEM HAVE TO BE THIS BEACON OF MACRONUTRIENT HOPE.'

Bloody love a good fritter, but fuck me there are a few trash recipes out there for them. I, too, am responsible for making some rough ones in my time that just fell apart or tasted like poorly thought out ideas. I went on that fucken bananas keto diet once and ate zucchini fritters every day for a month 'cause it was seemingly the only green vegetable I could eat without going over my carb allowance. Spent the whole month hating life and shitting myself. Worst. Anyway, these are bloody awesome and the flour in them means not only are they going to stick together properly, but they're also incidentally going to launch you lovingly out of ketosis in a rocket ship full of flavours.

SERVES: 3–4
COOKING TIME: around 30 mins
HECTOMETER: 3/10

INGREDIENTZZZ

500 G ZUCCHINI
SALT
225 G PACK HALOUMI
½ CUP SELF-RAISING FLOUR
½ CUP CHOPPED BASIL
1 EGG, LIGHTLY BEATEN
PEPPER
½ TEASPOON CHILLI FLAKES,
   OR 1 FRESH RED CHILLI, DESEEDED
   AND FINELY CHOPPED (OPTIONAL)
EXTRA VIRGIN OLIVE OIL TO SHALLOW FRY
   (5 MM DEEP OF OIL SHOULD GET YOU
   ACROSS THE LINE)
CORIANDER LEAVES, TO SERVE (OPTIONAL)

SALAD

1 DESEEDED LEBANESE CUCUMBER
1 TOMATO
RED ONION

GARLIC YOGHURT

1 CUP GREEK-STYLE YOGHURT
1 LEMON, ZESTED
1 GARLIC CLOVE, PEELED

EGG BASTARD

Some of the devices that are supposed to help you make food are fucken nothing short of hilarious. I was introduced to one of them by my mate Adam. It's called the Egg Master (I affectionately call it the Egg Bastard), a greased-up cylindrical device that you're supposed to crack eggs into and wait until they shit their cooked selves out the top. Absolutely putrid garbage. It even comes with a recipe book to make groundbreaking delicacies such as the 'egg dog', a hotdog-style thing but instead of meat you place one of these heinous egg logs in a bun. Who the fuck is eating that?

I took one with me as part of my tour and it would always get the biggest laughs when I brought it out on stage. It even makes this 'thonk' noise when you pull the sausage of cooked egg out of the machine. We had to cook them in the Egg Bastard thing before the show, but quickly learned that if you make them in the green room then the whole fucken room smells like someone dropped their guts. We even tried making them in the hotel bathroom with the fan on, but nope, it totally fucked the hotel room up, too. For days.

I'm all for making things easy in the kitchen, but trying to clean an electrical tube filled with old eggs and oil is not exactly what I would consider convenient. If you want to buy an actually sick cheating device that genuinely fucken kicks arse as well as makes things easier, get around the almighty sous vide. It's a simple gadget you can clip to a saucepan that heats up the water inside to a consistent temperature usually below 100°C. It's amazing at perfectly cooking meat through, and reheating things to exact temperatures. I bought a shitload of them for my family and friends for Christmas and they have all gone off as gifts. Look 'em up, champions.

If you feel the need to cook eggs in a device that looks like a Fleshlight, then all power to you, but may I suggest that it isn't as convenient as it seems and it makes your house smell like an arse.

SPICY PANTS SHAKSHUKA
(BUSH DOOF RESCUE)

Shakshuka is one of those fucken brekkie all-timers. Whether you're trying to impress someone with your seemingly wild 'dinner for breakfast' moves, or blow the minds of your hungover mates at a bush doof with this one-pan wonder, shakkas has got the lot. Seriously, you can even make this on a camp stove rather than eating another load of punishingly over-spiced curry out of a paper bowl. Don't do that . . . do this.

SERVES: 3–4
COOKING TIME: 30–40 mins
HECTOMETER: 3/10

RIGHTY'O JOE.

GRAB A BUNCH OF CORIANDER (OR PARSLEY IF YOU HATE CORIANDER, YA WEIRDO), CUT THE HAIRY ARSE OFF IT, THEN ROUGHLY CUT THE STALK PART AWAY FROM THE FOLIAGE PART UP THE TOP. KEEP THE LEAFY BIT ASIDE AND CHOP THE STALKS UP (THAT'S RIGHT, CHOP THE STALKS) AND BANG THEM IN THE SAME BOWL AS THE ONIONS AND CAPSICUM.

PEEL AND DICE THE RED ONION, DE-SEED THE CAPSICUM, DICE IT UP AND BANG ALL THAT SHIT IN A BOWL TOGETHER.

THEN COMES THE BIT THAT ALWAYS MAKES EVERYONE SAY THAT CLICHÉ, 'WOW THAT SMELLS AMAZING, WHAT ARE YOUUUUU COOOOKIIINNNNGGG?' TO WHICH YOU CAN REPLY... AGAIN, 'OH, THAT'S PROBABLY THE GARLIC' BECAUSE AT THIS POINT YOU WILL HAVE ADDED YOUR GARLIC AND CHILLI TO THE PAN, AND THAT'S GREAT 'CAUSE WE NEED TO COOK THAT NOW, AS WELL AS THE PAPRIKA AND CAYENNE. GIVE IT ALL A STIR AND COOK FOR A MINUTE OR TWO.

INTO THE PAN GO YOUR TINS OF WHOLE TOMATOES, BREAKING THEM APART WITH A WOODEN SPOON LIKE A COUPLE OF HIPPIE TOURISTS ARGUING OVER WHETHER BYRON BAY HAS SOLD OUT TO THE POINT OF BEING UNCOOL NOW. HALF-FILL ONE OF THE EMPTIED TOMATO CANS WITH WATER AND THEN, ODDLY ENOUGH, TIP THAT INTO THE OTHER EMPTY TIN, THEREFORE RINSING BOTH OF THEIR REMAINING TOMATOEYNESS TOGETHER AS YOU TIP ALL THAT PRATTLE-ON INTO THE PAN AS WELL.

FLICK IN A TEASPOON OF BROWN SUGAR ALONG WITH A PINCH OF SALT AND A CRACK OF PEPPER. TRY NOT TO GO TOO HARD ON THE SALT, 'CAUSE THERE'S NO COMING DOWN OFF THAT HIGH EASILY.

TURN THE HEAT RIGHT DOWN AND SIMMER SIMMER YA BIG WINNER FOR 15 MINUTES, OR ENOUGH TIME TO PUMP OUT A CUPPLA EYE-WATERINGLY BAD BEN HARPER COVERS ON THE MELODEON, LIKELY WITH SOME GUITAR-TAPPING ARSEHOLE CALLED WISH WHO CAN'T DECIDE WHETHER HE'S A GUITARIST, SHIT DRUMMER OR ASCENDING TO ANOTHER DIMENSION FULL OF ANNOYING FUCKWITS LIKE HIM.

AFTER THAT WHOLE SCENE HAS ENDED, BUNG 4-6 DING-HOLES INTO THE SAUCE AND CRACK YA EGGS DIRECTLY INTO THEM, SO THE THICKENED SAUCE STOPS THE EGG FROM RUNNING EVERYWHERE.

COOK THAT FOR ANOTHER 10 MINUTES ON LOW WITH A LID ON IT UNTIL THE EGGS ARE COOKED, OR BETTER YET – IF YOU HAPPEN TO BE AT A PLACE OF RESIDENCE THAT HAS BOTH A SHOWER AND A FUCKEN OVEN - CRANK THE OVEN TO 200°C FAN-FORCED (OR 220°C NON FANINATED), FANG IT IN THAT SHIT INSTEAD FOR 10 AND GO HAVE A SHOWER AND TAKE A LONG HARD LOOK AT YOURSELF, YA PEST.

ONCE THE EGGS LOOK FUCKEN
COOKED ENOUGH FOR YOUR
COOKED HEAD, THROW A BIT OF
THE LEFTOVER
CORIANDER/PARSLEY LEAVES
OVER IT WITH SOME FETA,
SERVE IT WITH SOME TRENDY
SOURDOUGH TOAST OR JUST
FUCKEN BREAD. FUCK IT, EVEN
SLAM ON A BIT OF HOT SAUCE
IF YOU'RE NOT SCARED OF
ANOTHER VISIT TO THAT
HARROWING COMPOSTING
TOILET FULL OF SAWDUST,
SHAME AND BAD MEMORIES UP
ON THE HILL.

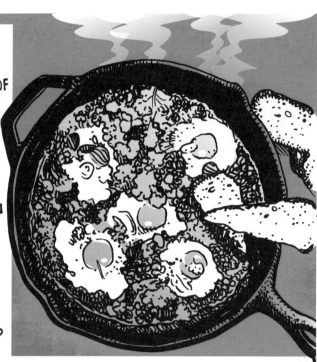

BURNIE
McLAVAPANTS
HOT SAUCE

A DISH SO GOOD
IT WILL EVEN
OFFER YOUR
SHATTERED ARSE
A RIDE HOME
FROM THE DOOF.

STUFF THAT GOES WITH OTHER SHIT

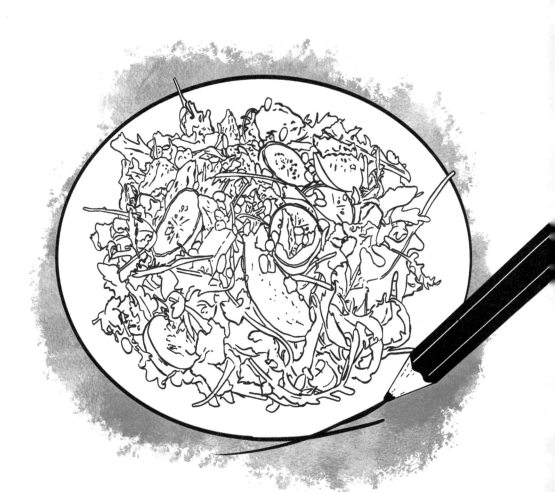

(NOT EVEN SHIT)
RAD SALAD

Fucken hell, haven't we all suffered a plethora of heinous salads in our lives that either tasted as if they crawled out of a lawn mower's arse or like someone tipped five tonnes of airline-food-level vinaigrette on a tree. It's fair enough that the word 'salad' often strikes bored fear into the hearts of many. Well I've had a gutful of living life in the grass lane! Let's change the game up and make a salad that doesn't make you want to put your head in your hands and wish you'd made almost anything else on earth.

SERVES: 3–4
COOKING TIME: less than 30 mins
HECTOMETER: 3/10

INGREDIENTS

75 G PINE NUTS
150 G ROCKET LEAVES
2 LEBANESE CUCUMBERS, SLICED THINLY
1 PEACH, DESTONED AND CHOPPED
150 G GOAT'S CHEESE, CRUMBLED
1 TABLESPOON EXTRA-VIRGIN OLIVE OIL
1 AVOCADO, SLICED

DRESSING

PINCH SEA SALT FLAKES
CRACK OF PEPPER
1-2 TABLESPOONS WARM WATER
⅔ TABLESPOON DIJON MUSTARD
1 TABLESPOON BALSAMIC VINEGAR
50 ML EXTRA-VIRGIN OLIVE OIL

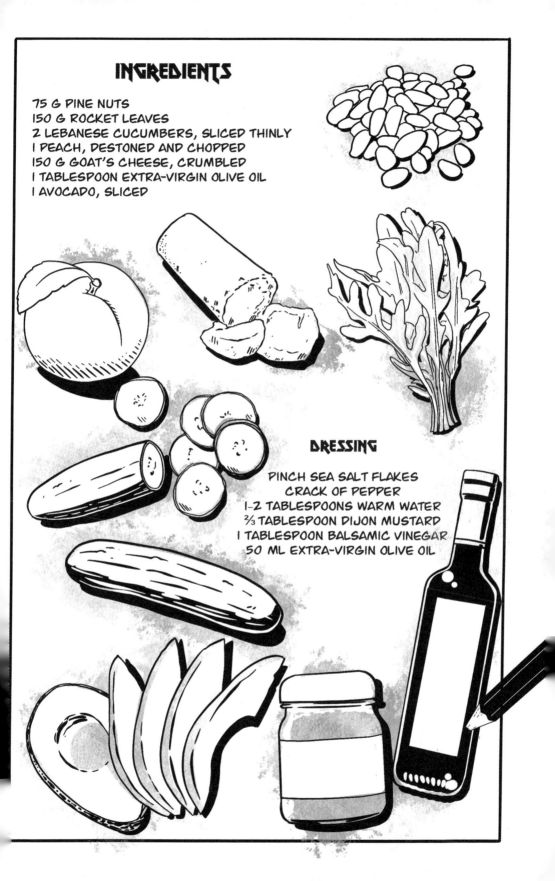

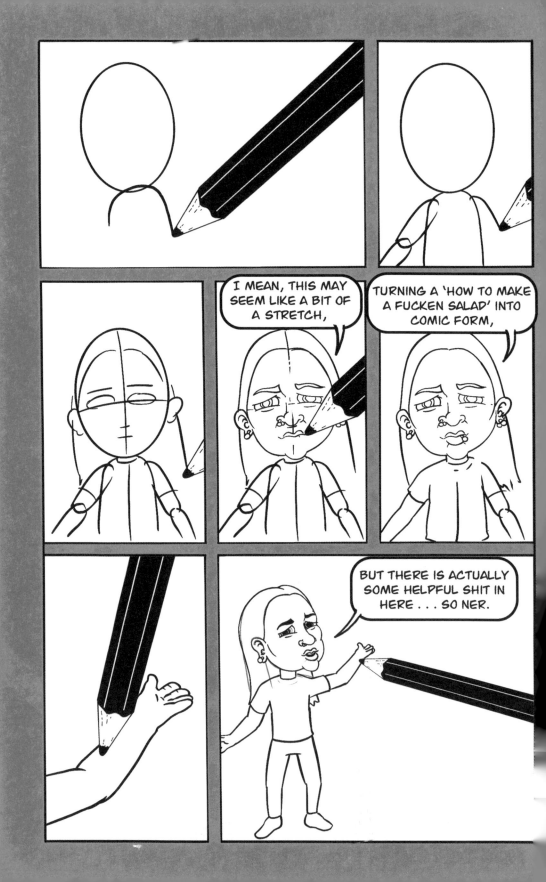

LET'S START WITH THE PINE NUTS. YOU MAY NEED TO REMORTGAGE YOUR HOUSE TO AFFORD THEM, BUT YOU DON'T NEED HEAPS. LET ME EXPLAIN WHAT TOASTING PINE NUTS DOES AND DOESN'T MEAN: IT DOESN'T MEAN DUMP THEM INTO THE FUCKEN TOASTER,

'CAUSE THAT SHIT WON'T WORK (THOUGH IT WILL SMELL NICE TRYING TO COOK THEM LIKE THIS, EVEN IF IT MAY ROYALLY FUCK YOUR TOASTER).

GET YOURSELF A NICE FLAT-BOTTOMED FRYING PAN, AND BUNG IT OVER A MEDIUM-HIGH HEAT.

NOW, DON'T PUT ANY OIL IN THE THING 'CAUSE THIS BIT OF THE RECIPE DOESN'T EVEN NEED IT.

ONCE THE PAN IS WARM, FANG IN THE PINE NUTS AND ROLL THEM AROUND UNTIL THEY JUST START TO TURN A TOUCH BROWN. THEY SHOULD SMELL INSANELY RAD TOO, WHICH IS GREAT 'CAUSE THIS IS A RAD SALAD.

ONCE YOU'VE HIT THAT POINT OF SEMI TOASTEDNESS, TURN THE HEAT OFF, TIP THEM FROM THE PAN INTO A BOWL AND SET ASIDE.

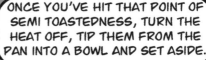

I MEAN, THERE'S NOT A GREAT DEAL HERE THAT YOU NEED TO KNOW OTHER THAN HOW TO MAKE THE DRESSING. THIS SALAD HAS ENOUGH GOING ON THAT YOU SHOULDN'T NEED TO DROWN THE FUCK OUT OF IT WITH 4 LITRES OF DRESSING – IN FACT, THAT APPROACH SHITS ME TO TEARS. IF I WANTED TO GO FOR A SWIM I WOULD BE WEARING MY SPEEDOS RIGHT NOW.

THIS DRESSING IS JUST ENOUGH TO TIP ITS HAT TO THE INGREDIENTS WITHOUT SHAKING YOU BY THE SHOULDERS WITH DEMANDS OF MORE FLAVOUR.

IT'S ACTUALLY A COOL WAY TO KEEP IT LIGHT AND GET ALL THE FLAVOURS TO HANG TOGETHER BEFORE YOU ADD YOUR OIL.

WATER SOUNDS LIKE A WEIRD INGREDIENT,

IS IT SHIT?

SALAD

Salad as a whole isn't going to get very many people shitting themselves with excitement for a fairly good reason – a lot of salads are indeed fucken wet trash, but certainly not all of them. That salad before is a ripper example of what I'm on about. It's not just a bunch of leaves swimming in over sweetened horse shit, it has varied ingredients and textures that complement each other. Salad has a bad rap because it's often served as a throwaway side, frequently at a café or restaurant as a way of making you feel as though you ate something healthy with your massive slab of microwave-reheated lasagne and extra large milkshake chaser. The little shitty bowl of garden salad drowned in 300 calories of vinaigrette has a lot to answer for in that respect. To me, it's like halfheartedly attending a healthy-themed dress-up party where the salad is a kind of cheap, badly fitting costume that's supposed to convince everyone the person underneath has come as a healthy person . . . but no one is buying it.

I think a lot of people look to salad for three things:

1. A way of correcting an otherwise grim diet.

2. A low calorie meal.

3. A way to turn leaves into a meal.

While it is possible to kiiiiinnnnnd of do all that, a lot of food describing itself as salad isn't actually that healthy – and it doesn't heaps need to be either, in my opinion. Not all dishes with green shit in them have to be this beacon of macronutrient hope, nor are they supposed to be some weight-loss powerhouse. Salad fucken rules if you look at it from a different angle, as it can be an opportunity to add some awesome shit to your plate and play around with a huge profile of sweet and savoury flavours all at once.

If you look outside the normal settings of the dish – lettuce, cucumber, tomato etc. – you can create a fucking banger of a feed. For me, goat's cheese paired with peach or nectarine has been an absolute weapon in the fight against mundanity. Rather than tipping 50,000 kalamata olives into a lettuce-filled bowl with whatever the fuck 'French dressing' is and stirring it together till it looks like a fucken beach covered in washed-up old weeds, try finding a few of your favourite salady things and building flavours from there without needing to drown it in jar sauce-level dressing to make it exciting enough to eat. A few ingredients can make an otherwise boring salad fucken awesome I reckon, and it won't even be shit.

Not shit.

'DON'T BE A FUCKWIT AT THE SHOPS AND GO SQUASHING THE FUCK OUT OF ALL THE AVOCADOS. IF IT FEELS A LITTLE SOFT, YOU'RE PROBABLY GOOD TO GO.'

GET FUCKED
ROAST POTATOES

Now, I know what you're thinking. 'Are you telling me to get fucked and then just saying roast potatoes?' No, I'm not; I'm merely suggesting that this way of cooking potatoes is so good you'll say 'get fucked' after eating them, or just want to tell everyone to 'get fucked' so you can have them all to yourself. A good roast potato is such an amazing thing, and there are a few cheeky little tricks that will make a huge difference to your taters.

SERVES: 4–6 as a side
COOKING TIME: around 1.5 hours
HECTOMETER: 2/10

THE REASON IS 'CAUSE THE POTATOES COOK MORE EVENLY THIS WAY, AND WE LIKE TO KEEP THINGS EVEN, STEPHEN.

I KNEW THAT!

STEPHEN KING THE SPUD

BRING THE COLD WATER TO A VERY UN-COLD BOIL AND COOK THE POTATO FOR ABOUT 10-15 MINUTES DEPENDING ON THE SIZE OF THESE BAD BOIZ. WE WANT THEM TENDER BUT NOT AN OVERCOOKED POT OF MEALY RUBBISH. GENTLY STICK IN A FORK OR THE TIP OF A KNIFE TO READ THE VIBE.

GO WITH YOUR GUTS ON THIS ONE..

IT'S DONE!

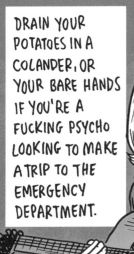

DRAIN YOUR POTATOES IN A COLANDER, OR YOUR BARE HANDS IF YOU'RE A FUCKING PSYCHO LOOKING TO MAKE A TRIP TO THE EMERGENCY DEPARTMENT.

IT IS NOW MY DUTY TO COMPLETELY DRAIN YOU.

LET THEM REST AND STEAM OUT FOR A FEW MINUTES. WHILE THEY ARE TAKING IT EASY, POUR A GOOD BELT OF OLIVE OIL INTO THE ROASTING TRAY, AND WHACK IT IN THE OVEN.

BRUTAL FOOD COMPLIMENTS

Seems strange to tell someone where to go when you just had the first mouthful of a meal they lovingly prepared for you, but sometimes you just can't help yourself 'cause it just tastes so damn good. Bit weird, isn't it, that when something is so great you need to drop some hectic sentence to let the world know just how amazing you feel about it at that moment?

✖ 'Fuck off, this is amazing!'
✖ 'Don't talk to me right now. This is too awesome.'
✖ 'This needs to calm down, you need to calm down with this tasty shit.'

And one of my faves:
✖ 'This doesn't even suck.'

Like you're almost upset with how great it all is but not even upset about it at all – in fact you're just loving it sick. We are a strange lot, aren't we? I've definitely had people say 'fuck you' for making food that they loved, and I was so totally fine with it. Language is funny like that, how negative-sounding words can also double as compliments of the highest order. Seemingly the more brutal the comments are, the more kudos they offer. There's an art to it for sure, though – you can't just keep telling the person who made dinner to fuck off or it might be the last meal they ever make for you.

Like anything, practice makes perfect, so if something is just that earth-shatteringly good that you need to tell the whole room to fuck off 'cause you're having such a fabulous time, then so be it. Get fucked, you're an amazing cook.

INCIDENTALLY VEGAN STREET COLESLAW

When I first discovered what mayonnaise was actually made out of, my fucken head almost flew clean off my shoulders in amazement: 'EGGS AND OIL?' I said to my dad. 'Yes,' he replied.

There are so many incredible dishes out there that are just as good, if not better, when made as vegan. This here is a champagne example of exactly that; you don't need even the eggs to make a righteous mayo and I'll prove it to ya. The liquid that your canned chickpeas float around in is the replacement for the eggs, and believe it or not it goes off like a vegan frog in a sock.

SERVES: 4–6 as a side
COOKING TIME: 30–45 mins
HECTOMETER: 4/10

INGREDIENTS

- 400 G TIN CHICKPEAS, DRAINED BUT LIQUID RESERVED FOR THE MAYO
- 2 TABLESPOONS EXTRA VIRGIN OLIVE OIL
- SALT
- $\frac{1}{2}$ TEASPOON FINELY GROUND BLACK PEPPER
- 1 TEASPOON CHILLI FLAKES
- $\frac{1}{4}$ RED CABBAGE
- $\frac{1}{4}$ WHITE CABBAGE
- 1 SMALL RED ONION, PEELED
- 1 LARGE CARROT, PEELED
- 1 TEASPOON CELERY OR SESAME SEEDS, CRUSHED

VEGAN MAYO
- 2 TEASPOONS DIJON MUSTARD
- $\frac{1}{3}$ CUP AQUAFABA (THE LIQUID FROM A CHICKPEA CAN)
- 2 TEASPOONS APPLE CIDER VINEGAR
- 300 ML VEGETABLE OIL
- JUICE OF HALF LEMON
- SEA SALT FLAKES

AFTER DINNER MINTS

TIRAMEEZOO

If you are wondering who the flip Jim is, it's worth a dig through the back catalogue of my channel to find some of the weirdest face-swapping (and at times rubber mask) character videos I've made. Let me tell ya, those Jim videos can get pretty fucken cooked at times. I developed him as a representation of the classic old Aussie fella who likes the simple things in life, and at the same time he's a little eccentric and has a habit of getting a little carried away . . . my future, I'm sure.

If there is one thing I know about Jim, it's that he loves a coffee or forty, as well as the occasional scoop of Blue Ribbon. He has been known at times to fondly combine those two flavours in a word he pronounces with his oh-so-Australian timbre: 'tirameeezoooo'. As an homage to the great man himself, here is a ripper of a tiramisu that he would be more than happy to put away all by himself.

SERVES: 8
COOKING TIME: under an hour
(resting time: a few hours to overnight)
HECTOMETER: 6/10

ONCE COOL, WHISK IN THE VANILLA AND MASCARPONE (THE ONLY CHEESE USED TO HIDE A HORSE). ALL THAT NONSENSE, INCLUDING THAT SHIT HORSE JOKE, CAN CONTINUE TO RELAX FOR A BIT WHILE YOU GET ON WITH YOUR COMEDY CAREER AND THE REST OF THE DISH.

POUR THE CREAM INTO A LARGE BOWL. NOW COMES THE TIME TO GET THAT ARM OF YOURS READY (OR QUICKLY RUN OUT AND BUY AN ELECTRIC MIXER) AND WHISK THE ABSOLUTE ENDLESS FUCK OUT OF THE CREAM, WHICH AS I'VE MENTIONED IN OTHER PARTS OF THIS BOOK TAKES WAY LONGER THAN IT SHOULD, BUT DOES- TRUST ME- GET THERE IN THE END. THE CREAM SEEMINGLY OUT OF NOWHERE WILL FORM NICE THICK PEAKS, AT WHICH TIME YOU MAY NEED A SHOULDER RECONSTRUCTION, BUT IT'S ALSO A GREAT TIME TO FOLD THE CREAM INTO THE HORSE JOKE BOWL OF MASCARPONE FROM EARLIER.

NOW, SOME COFFEE IS NEEDED. HOWEVER YOU CHOOSE TO GET THERE IS UP TO YOU. I DON'T WANT TO HAVE TO GROW A BEARD AND TIE A TOP KNOT AND GET INTO A WHOLE BARISTA THING HERE ABOUT 'WHAT KIND OF FUCKEN COFFEE TO USE' 'CAUSE I DON'T REALLY GIVE A SPECIAL FUCK. JUST AS LONG AS IT'S 1½ CUPS OF STRONG BLACK COFFEE (AND NO, A SHITTY ICED COFFEE FROM THE SERVO WILL NOT DO THE TRICK, CHAMP).

ONCE YOU'VE NAVIGATED THAT JOURNEY, MAGELLAN, ADD THE REMAINING ¼ CUP OF SUGAR TO IT AND TIP THE SWEET COFFEE INTO A SHALLOW BOWL FOR COOL REASONS THAT IT NEEDS TO COOL OFF. COOL? ONCE IT'S TOO COOL FOR SCHOOL, STIR IN THE MARSALA OR FRANGELICO.

YOU RIFLING THROUGH YOUR CUPBOARD AND SUDDENLY FINDING A 22 CM SQUARE DISH IS FANTASTIC NEWS FOR US ALL RIGHT NOW, 'CAUSE WE WILL USE IT. SPREAD ABOUT A THIRD OF THE HORSE HIDER INTO THE BOTTOM OF THE DISH, THEN WITH YOUR HANDS OR TONGS IF YOU HAVE A GENTLE TOUCH, DIP THE BICKIES INTO THE COFFEE MIXTURE- DIP FAST 'CAUSE NEITHER THE BICKIES NOR THE COFFEE WILL LAST. THEN ARRANGE THEM OVER THE MASCARPONE UNTIL YOU'VE CREATED A LAYER.

NOW DUST OVER SOME COCOA WITH A SIEVE, COVER IT WITH HALF OF THE REMAINING HORSE HIDER AND ANOTHER LAYER OF COFFEE-DIPPED BICKIES FOLLOWED BY MORE COCOA POWDER. TOP ALL THAT WITH THE REMAINING CREAM MIXTURE, SMOOTH OUT THE TOP LAYER AND AGAIN DUST WITH MORE COCOA.

LAYERS OF GOODNESS

COCOA DUSTIN'

MASCARPONE

COCOA DUSTIN'

COFFEE BICKIES

MASCARPONE

COCOA DUSTIN'

COFFEE BICKIES

THIN LAYER MASCARPONE

A DAY IN THE LIFE OF JIM

Jim is a creature of habit. He wakes at 4.30 am to the alarm clock radio that is set so obnoxiously fucken loud it could give any normal person a tan in their ear drums. He then throws on his brown dressing gown and Bundy brand slippers, flaps out to the kitchen, cranks the fuck out of the radio in there as well, but this time to a different station because he likes to be across both news channels since his politics lie somewhere in between the two.

The whole house now sounds like what can only be described as a busy punters' lounge. The neighbours slam their windows shut as they yell, 'For fuck's sake, Jim, do you have to fucken have it up so loud, mate?!' Jim can't hear that because he doesn't give a fuck. He then wanders down the hallway out to the back garage through the flyscreen door. He has to kick the shit out of the bottom of it 'cause the fucken thing is fucked and it's the only way to get it to open. The sound of his kicking the door sets off the birds in the backyard, and soon enough he's heading out across the lawn to the chest freezer in the back garage to get his frozen Shape milk for his coffees.

Jim keeps the milk out the back in the deep freeze because it lasts longer that way, and there's no room in the front fridge for the 16 litres he goes through a week. He drinks Shape milk because it's got a picture of a thin person on the milk bottle, and Jim is convinced that since drinking this milk he has dropped a shitload of kgs. What's more, recently the doc gave him the heads-up that the 2 litres of whole milk and entire tub of Blue Ribbon he was going through every day had a shitload of calories in them and were giving him a 'bit of a gut'.

He makes his way back to the kitchen to put the milk in the microwave to defrost. He usually spends about 5 minutes making loud, repetitive beeping noises on the microwave keypad, trying to program the fucken defrost setting but constantly messing it up and having to try again. This amount of noise, along with Jim swearing loudly at it, further pisses off the neighbours. The fella next door opens his window and yells at Jim, 'Come on Jimmo, give it a fucken rest, would ya?' Jim keeps beeping away as he tries to program the weight of the milk into the microwave and eventually gives up and just uses the max setting.

Jim then fills up the stovetop kettle and places it on the heat. The kettle is one of those that whistles loudly when it's ready, of course. It takes about the same amount of time to boil as the milk takes to defrost in the microwave.

He goes to fetch a teaspoon from the top drawer, which is so stiff and hard to open that he has to yank it the fuck out with all his strength until it comes crashing open and all the cutlery makes an enormous clang.

The kettle begins to boil and whistle, as does Jim; he loves to try and harmonise in a duet with the kettle's whistle. This goes on for a minute as he finally gives it up and turns the heat off.

With the spoon he has fetched from the drawer he pops the lid off the tin of international roast, which lands with a clang on the counter. He scoops 4 heaped teaspoons into his mug, followed by the hot water and a healthy dash of Shape. From the pantry, Jim fetches the Promite and Tip Top White Toast loaf. He makes himself some medium-rare toast with Promite, takes the lot out to the lounge and places it on the coffee table.

To add to the haunting chorus of several types of news reports blaring throughout the house, Jim switches on the national news and competes to get it louder than everything else.

Jim soaks up as much info as he can before midday, and drinks about ten–twelve cups of coffee as a rule.

At about lunchtime he makes the pivot to the teas and mows the lawn. The lawn is mowed every day, mostly because Jim finds the sound of the mower calming and needs to shake off the thousands of milligrams' worth of caffeinated energy somehow. He then spends a few hours watching *Days of Our Lives* and *The Price Is Right* re-runs until beer o'clock.

Come about 3 pm it's time for a beer. There is only one beer in this house and that's Light Ice. Jim has stockpiled an absurd amount of it in the garage from years ago and doesn't care that it's gone off. He spent a lot of money on it at the time and he isn't going to fucken waste it. Jim puts away a couple of beers and makes the move to dinner ale as a nod to what's to come.

When dinnertime comes around, the radios are both turned off and Jim eats his favourite meal of the day in front of the TV: dim sims with tomato sauce, paired with a side of frozen mixed veg garnished with a tablespoon of margarine and a sprinkle of table salt.

Jim stays up to watch *Four Corners* clutching a bowl of Blue Ribbon with a sprinkling of Milo and instant coffee on top, then it's off to bed.

It's a big day tomorrow and the Shape isn't gonna fucken drink itself.

WAKE AND
DON'T BAKE
ORANGE & LEMON
CHEESECAKE

I have memories of eating cheesecake at a shitty shopping-centre café as a kid and trying to forget the word 'cheese' while I ate it. Definitely a little confused as to how it fucking had actual 'cheese' in it? I was. I mean it does, but it's not the kind of cheese I was thinking of back then. I think I pictured a Kraft Single with sprinkles on it and a lit candle popped on top, or something. I've since learned how the magic happens there and I'm sure it helps that I'm not seven years old anymore, which is great news for us all, as otherwise this book would be full of ice cream and Fruit Loops recipes.

No-bake cheesecake was Jules' idea, by the way – a ripper one it is too. The shit is so easy to make, particularly my way. I mean it when I say 'don't bake' . . . like you don't need to do.

SERVES: 8

COOKING TIME: under 30 mins to not even cook; resting time: 4+ hours

HECTOMETER: 3/10

INGREDIENTS

CHEESE SINGLES AND ICE MAGIC (JUST KIDDING)

ACTUAL INGREDIENTS

1 ORANGE (HALF FOR JUICE, ONE FOR ZEST)
2 LEMONS (TWO FOR JUICE, ONE FOR ZEST)
200 G SCOTCH FINGER OR DIGESTIVE BICKIES
100 G BUTTER, PLUS EXTRA FOR GREASING
500 G CREAM CHEESE, AT ROOM TEMPERATURE (BLOCK FORM,
   NOT SPREADABLE)
140 G CASTER SUGAR
1 CUP THICKENED CREAM
1 TEASPOON GROUND DUTCH CINNAMON, OR JUST NORMAL SHIT

GEAR

20CM-ISH ROUND
   SPRINGFORM CAKE TIN

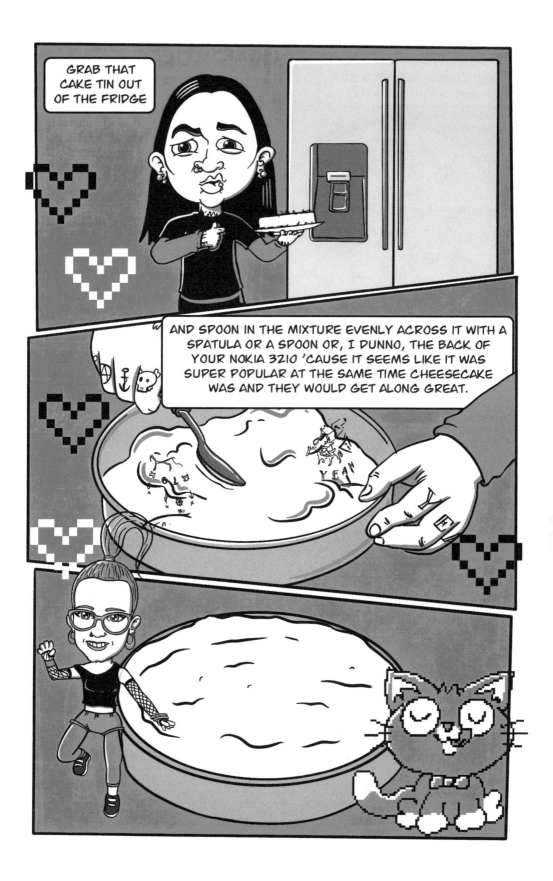

'IF IT DOESN'T
COME OUT LOOKING
PERFECT,
IT DOESN'T BLOODY
PARRAMATTA.'

FROWNIE
REVERSAL
ORANGE
CHOCOLATE
BROWNIE

Brownies and orange-flavoured chocolate each
have a reputation for being simultaneously
awesome and indulgent, and, to be fair,
a little old school, too. I remember orange
chocolate being one of those things that
would blow my little fucken mind as a kid,
while pumping my lolly bag at the cinema
full of enough Jaffas to frighten most parents.
I have vivid memories of thinking that
every time I ate chocolate with orange in it,
those were probably some of the best
times of my fucken life. So let's make
memories and blow minds with the
best fucken brownie in town.
(PS If you don't like orange chocolate,
just don't put the orange in the brownie, lol.)

SERVES: 6–8 solid doses
COOKING TIME: a bit over an hour
HECTOMETER: 4/10

INGREDIENTS

- 1 large (or 2 small) oranges, zest only
- 200g butter
- 100g dark chocolate, go as dark or as less dark as you like, 70%+ seems to go pretty good, broken into pieces
- 1 cup plain flour
- 1/3 cup cocoa powder
- 1/2 teaspoon baking powder
- pinch of salt
- 1 cup caster sugar
- 1 cup brown sugar
- 4 eggs, lightly beaten
- 2 teaspoons vanilla bean paste or vanilla extract

NOW WE'RE OFF TO THE RACES GROOVER. TIP ALL THAT RADNESS GENTLY INTO THE TRAY, SPREAD IT OUT EVEN STEPHEN AND BUNG IT IN THE OVEN FOR 45 MINUTES OR UNTIL JUST SET IN THE CENTRE.

A GOOD WAY TO TELL IS TO GIVE IT A GENTLE SHAKE — THE ULTIMATE BROWNIE CONSISTENCY IS COMPLETELY SET ON THE EDGES WITH A SLIGHT LIDDLE JIGGLE IN THE MIDDLE.

SHIT FOOD, BUT SO GOOD

When I was a kid, I swore the fucken second I was old enough to buy my own food I was never gonna eat anything else except ice cream and lollies. I remember giving it a solid run for its pocket money even well into my teenage years. A strict diet of soft drinks and food from the corner store really had legs. I went absolutely bananas on that shit till I made myself fucking sick as a dog. It is a testament to the younger human body and what it can survive on at that age – I swear to fucken god for a whole year I only ate servo pies and takeaway pizza, drank cola exclusively and smoked heaps of weed. A real hero's diet. I have these memories of holding my stomach, super confused as to what the fuck was wrong and why I felt so fucking crook . . . To nobody's surprise, what I was experiencing was what I've come to learn is either heartburn or indigestion . . . or both.

Now that I appreciate what actual food is, I know that eating like a massive fuckwit makes you feel like shit.

But that's not to say I don't have some fucking old-school shit food favourites that I will dip my toe in the heartburn pool for on occasion even now, and love it sick.

The top five indigestion starters I will fucken still destroy at the drop of a hat:

1. THE SAUSAGE SIZZLE

I find it near impossible to not lose my absolute fucken mind at the smell, sight or even sound of a sausage sizzle. I'll even excuse shitty white bread and margarine for that hot second. Sure, there are classier ways to consume this food, but it's hard to argue with the shit sausage, oily fried onion, white bread and tomato sauce combo and how amazing that level of radness is. You can't even go to Bunnings anymore without being targeted by this evil genius.

2. BURGER WITH THE LOT

A fucken classic Aussie hit that is borderline too big for your mouth, but that's pretty much what makes it so fucken good. The meat has to be flattened out as fuck and kinda taste like mysteries, and the bizarre pineapple ring, egg and beetroot party gets me every time.

3. THE MUSK STICK

A very bloody strange one, I know. It's a hard pink candy stick that tastes like perfume . . . and I love it. I have lost a few people on this one before, not heaps of you on my side here. I even almost lost respect for myself when I looked up what musk was.

4. THE BACON AND EGG ROLL

It's the sausage sizzle of the breakfast world and a great way to start your guts off on the back foot for the entire day. Barbecue sauce probably doesn't help, either.

5. BOURBON AND COKE

Seriously not at all a classy drink by any means, yet it comes with such fond memories, even of hangovers so bad they have their own postcode.

I'm not too good for some shit food, I just value things that make me feel good and not shit myself. It's nice to know that I have other more dynamic culinary answers to my hunger questions these days.

'LET'S JUST SAY
THAT PAVS ARE
A LITTLE LIKE
SNOWFLAKES –
THEY ARE DELICATE
AND HAVE A RANGE
OF STRUCTURAL
INTEGRITY ISSUES.'

PAVLOVA
THE PATIENCE CAKE

I mean, do I really need to say anything here? It's a pav, for fuck's sake. This is the *BMX Bandits* of cakes: chockers full of what I'm sure are Chrissytime memories of being surrounded by punishing relatives you wish you could escape, as well as bizarre and often overly expressive fruit arrangements on what is more or less a giant meringue. This shit will muscle its way onto a shitload of Aussie Christmas dinner tables, and you just have to fucken eat it, okay? So let's make one that's actually so sick it probably wears a backwards Monster Energy hat and does backflips on a jet ski.

SERVES: 6–8
COOKING TIME: a few hours
HECTOMETER: 6/10

INGREDIENTS

6 EGG WHITES FROM XL EGGS (FROM A 700G BOX OF A DOZEN)

* IF YOU'RE USING SMALL EGGS, (SAY FROM A 550G DOZEN) THEN YOU NEED TO USE ANOTHER EGG WHITE.

1½ CUPS (330G) CASTER SUGAR, PLUS 1 TEASPOON FOR CREAM

2 TEASPOONS CORNFLOUR

1 TEASPOON WHITE VINEGAR

300 ML THICKENED CREAM

1 TEASPOON VANILLA EXTRACT OR VANILLA BEAN PASTE

FRUIT, TO SERVE

(BERRIES RULE BUT YOU CAN CHOOSE YOUR ADVENTURE)

CHOOSE YOUR FRUIT ADVENTURE

YOU'RE THE CHAMPION OF THE STORY!
CHOOSE FROM 22 POSSIBLE ENDINGS

FRUITS FOR THE PAVLOVA PLANET

BY NAT'S WHAT I RECKON

caster sugar

VINEGAR

THICKENED CREAM

ILLUSTRATED BY GLENNO

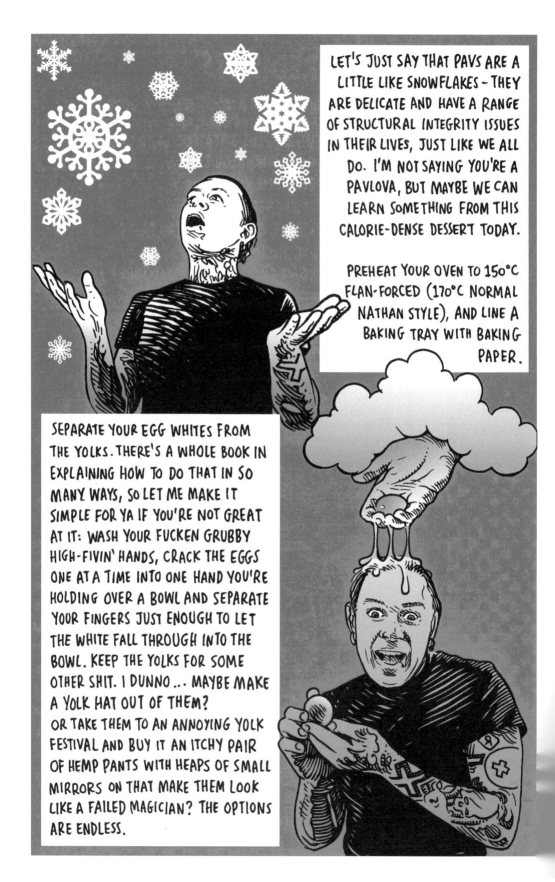

LET'S JUST SAY THAT PAVS ARE A LITTLE LIKE SNOWFLAKES – THEY ARE DELICATE AND HAVE A RANGE OF STRUCTURAL INTEGRITY ISSUES IN THEIR LIVES, JUST LIKE WE ALL DO. I'M NOT SAYING YOU'RE A PAVLOVA, BUT MAYBE WE CAN LEARN SOMETHING FROM THIS CALORIE-DENSE DESSERT TODAY.

PREHEAT YOUR OVEN TO 150°C FLAN-FORCED (170°C NORMAL NATHAN STYLE), AND LINE A BAKING TRAY WITH BAKING PAPER.

SEPARATE YOUR EGG WHITES FROM THE YOLKS. THERE'S A WHOLE BOOK IN EXPLAINING HOW TO DO THAT IN SO MANY WAYS, SO LET ME MAKE IT SIMPLE FOR YA IF YOU'RE NOT GREAT AT IT: WASH YOUR FUCKEN GRUBBY HIGH-FIVIN' HANDS, CRACK THE EGGS ONE AT A TIME INTO ONE HAND YOU'RE HOLDING OVER A BOWL AND SEPARATE YOUR FINGERS JUST ENOUGH TO LET THE WHITE FALL THROUGH INTO THE BOWL. KEEP THE YOLKS FOR SOME OTHER SHIT. I DUNNO... MAYBE MAKE A YOLK HAT OUT OF THEM?
OR TAKE THEM TO AN ANNOYING YOLK FESTIVAL AND BUY IT AN ITCHY PAIR OF HEMP PANTS WITH HEAPS OF SMALL MIRRORS ON THAT MAKE THEM LOOK LIKE A FAILED MAGICIAN? THE OPTIONS ARE ENDLESS.

NOW, WITH THE EGG WHITES WE HAVE A MISSION AHEAD. IF YOU DON'T HAVE A STAND MIXER OR AN ELECTRIC HANDHELD MIXER, THEN MAYBE CONSIDER BUYING SOME KIND OF GROWTH HORMONE AND START A SEVEN-DAYS-A-WEEK #NODAYSOFF STRENGTH-TRAINING REGIME FOR A FEW YEARS PRIOR TO BEGINNING THIS RECIPE, 'CAUSE YOUR FUCKEN ARM IS GONNA GET A WORK-OUT IF YOU USE A REGULAR WHISK, MUSCLES.

TRUST ME, I HAVE MADE THIS PAV WITH A WHISK BEFORE, AND WHILE IT IS POSSIBLE, I DO HAVE A HABIT OF FINDING THINGS OUT THE 'HARD WAY', AND THAT'S NOT OFTEN THE BEST WAY, SO FINDING EASIER ROUTES TO THIS DESTINATION SUCH AS BORROWING A BEATER/MIXER OF SOME SORT WOULD BE A SMART MOVE.

WHATEVER OPTION YOU'VE GONE FOR, YOU'RE GUNNA NEED TO WHISK/BEAT/HARD WAY THOSE EGG WHITES INTO SOFT PEAKS. GRADUALLY ADD THE SUGAR 1 TABLESPOON AT A TIME UNTIL YOUR ARM HAS FUCKEN CALLED THE COPS ON YOU, THEN IN GOES THE CORN FLOUR AND VINEGAR IN THE SAME MANNER. KEEP WHISKING TILL ALL THE FUCKEN BLOODY SUGAR HAS DISSOLVED.

IF YOU'RE WONDERING WHETHER YOUR BIG WHITE BOWL OF CALORIE CLOUDS HAS REACHED THIS STAGE, THEN USE YOUR FINGERS TO SQUEEZE A LITTLE BETWEEN THEM AND SEE WHETHER IT FEELS SANDY OR NOT, IT SHOULD'NT.

SPOON YOUR EFFORT INTO THE CENTRE OF THE PREPARED BAKING TRAY, USING A FORKLIFT, OR IF YOU DON'T HAVE ONE OF THOSE LYING AROUND THEN THE BACK OF A SPOON WILL HAVE TO DO IN ORDER TO SHAPE IT INTO A THING.

YOU WANT TO MAKE THIS PILE OF FLUFF LOOK LIKE A SHAPE THAT RESEMBLES SOMETHING ALONG THE LINES OF A SERIOUSLY DEEP DISH LARGE PIZZA. I SUPPOSE LIKE ALL FOOD THAT YOU CREATE, IT'S MODERATELY CONCEPTUAL SO THERE IS NO RIGHT OR WRONG WAY TO SHAPE IT SINCE IT DOESN'T REALLY AFFECT THE FLAVOUR. I LIKE TO IMAGINE THE CHEAP SUPERMARKET MUD CAKE KINDA SHAPE AND GO FOR THAT ... SEEMS TO WORK WELL.

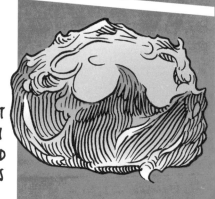

CHRISTMAS NONSENSE

To be quite honest, as someone who suffers with chronic anxiety, I'm not a huge fan of Christmas. But before I hang a stack of shit on it, I will say that I acknowledge that unlike a lot of people, I am lucky to be someone who has a place to go on the day if I want to, and I'm grateful for that.

Christmas Day is supposed to embody the tradition of togetherness with family and friends, where everyone is in great company and has a lovely old carefree time, and when you simply eat food and all feel so 'happy' to be around each other. But some Christmas get-togethers are often closer in vibe to a stressful wedding than to a happy celebration.

If we were to totally just cut the shit for a hot second and look at these consumerist tornados of holidays for what they are for some of us, we'd realise they seem like an excuse for a disorganised bunch of family who occasionally find each other's company tricky, to gather and trash some poor relative's house in the hope that they can all breathe out the woes of the year behind them. All the while spending a tonne of cash on a bunch of superfluous shit for each other, a gesture advertised in every way possible as a necessary way of demonstrating love and thoughtfulness.

And as someone who at times has also struggled with money, for reasons as wide-ranging as being on the dole to struggling to keep down a job, Christmas is stressful on your pocket, too. At this time of year when you have two families (like I do) and possibly heaps of fucken people coming over for the festivities, you can feel terrified, and almost certainly overwhelmed. Your sense of feeling like a broke deadshit is dialled up to 11. You're told that your company alone is enough, but inside it doesn't ever feel like enough. Every time someone gives you a present at the Chrissy get-together and you don't have anything to give back, you feel like a piece of shit . . .

Shall we have a plate of ham to go with our plummeting sense of self-worth, for some reason?

My point is that Christmas is one of those times of year that slams 'good vibes only' down your fucken throat and tells you to buckle up 'cause everyone is pumped for it, but ignores the fact that you might actually feel super down, and forced into keeping it together for everyone else's sake.

Of course, loving a day like Christmas Day is a wonderful thing, and not always problematic for everyone – but I feel for those of us who don't just breeze through it. If there is any chance in your life to experience happiness and joy, you should absolutely fucking go for it, champions. After all, Christmas is definitely that for a lot of people. I'm not trying to yuck people's yum here by any means, I'm merely saying that days that are supposedly the 'happiest time of the year', are sometimes some of the toughest to manage for others.

Like many days, Christmas Day demands something from the people who participate in it that isn't always beneficial for them. If you want to spend time with others, then I think you should, whereas if you prefer to set healthy boundaries around what keeps you well, then don't feel pressured by the Festive Industrial Complex into attending a hectic gathering.

Do what makes you happy.

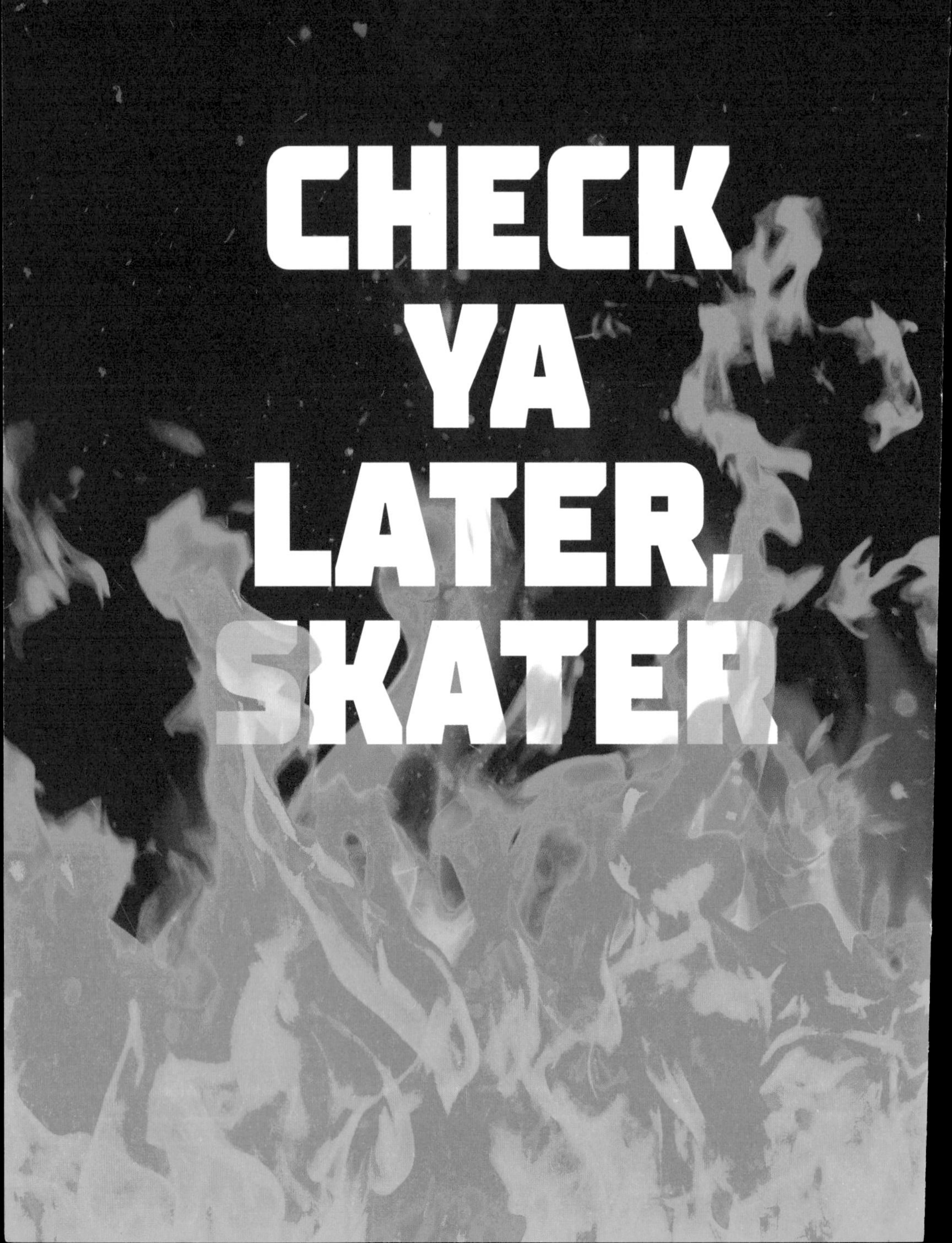
CHECK YA LATER, SKATER

Well, champignon, I hope you had a good time cruising through my recipe book and looking at all the pretty drawings, and, who knows, maybe you even cooked some of the food in it. I am very grateful you made it this far, even if you've only picked it up at the shops and leafed your way to the back to see whether it's gonna fucken do your head in or not.

If you had a crack at cooking one of the recipes in here and it didn't work out the way you'd planned, that's so okay. Give it another shot when you're feeling up to it – you'll nail it soon enough. I'm just grateful that you would trust me enough to buy all the ingredients to give it a go.

I hope you found ya new favourite feed in here, or I've helped you to discover a new dish that you really love cooking. I hope cooking your tucker has brought you together with some mates, family or selected family after a hard day in your head, and given you a moment off. Whatever it may be, I hope there is a win for you via a good feed. Cooking truly fucking rules, it just does.

Keep cooking for yourself and cooking for the people you love, you're all very much worth the effort.

Thanks for the hangs.

You're a bloody champion!

CONTRIBUTORS

Julia Gee

Jules is Nat's creative accomplice and cackle chorus on Nat's What I Reckon, as well as his off-screen partner in crime. A designer by trade, Jules is responsible for the channel's graphics and most merchandise designs, and can now add cinematographer extraordinaire and book co-conspirator to her assorted string of creative titles. When she's not getting artsy, she can often be found indulging her love of cheese and *RuPaul's Drag Race* (the two are inseparable), cuddling her house chickens (ragdoll cats), dancing (badly) or playing drums. Follow her behind-the-scenes adventures at ⓞ **@holy_bat_syllables** and her art at ⓞ **@housechickenstudios**.

Glenn 'Glenno' Smith

Glenno is a desk-bound art tradesman who feels both lucky to draw stuff for a living as well as driven nuts by the stuff he is asked to draw. (His fault for living in the most stupidly expensive place on earth and working with rock 'n' roll types.) His overachievements can be seen via ⓞ **@glennoart** and at **glennoart.com**. His amazing and beautiful wife is Gina, his weird cats are Roppongi, Panchetta and Koenji Greyjoy, and his bands are Chinese Burns Unit, Hellebores and Outcest.

Bunkwaa

Bunkwaa is an Australian comic book artist, animator and illustrator. His art is a sleight-of-hand journey into hyper-cartoon worlds, a kaleidoscopic ride full of character, worlds within worlds and faces within faces. You can connect with him at ⓞ **@bunkwaa** and learn more about his latest projects at **bunkwaa.com**.

Onnie O'Leary

Onnie O'Leary has been tattooing since 2011 after achieving a Bachelor of Visual Arts from Sydney College of the Arts in 2008. While her practice encompasses tattooing, print making, drawing, design and illustration, her focus is on graphic and brightly coloured pin-up style artwork, using geometric shapes to frame her work and eye-catching colour fades with a focus on traditional tattoo techniques to make these designs stand the test of time. Inspired by the erotic comic book styles of European artists in the 70s and 80s, she creates unique tattoos for clients both local and international. Onnie has been working at TLD Tattoo since 2017, and hopes to for many years to come. ⊙ **@onnieolearytattoo**

Warrick McMiles

Warrick McMiles is a proud Kamilaroi man, Australian artist, illustrator and tattooist based in Sydney's Inner West. From drawing his favourite cartoons as a kid, to graffiti as a teen, to being commissioned to produce murals all across Sydney, his influences include his world travels in the Royal Australian Navy, 80s and 90s pop culture and the street art and hip-hop scenes. You can find Warrick at the Something Original tattoo studio in Newtown, Sydney, Gadigal Country, and at ⊙ **@warrick_mcmiles.**

ACKNOWLEDGEMENTS

I have to firstly chuck a massive shout-out to the fucking insanely incredible artists who helped turn my ridiculous way of speaking in constant metaphor into incredibly funny and beautiful drawings. Onnie, Glenno, Warrick and Bunkwaa, you're my bloody heroes.

To Jules, my amazing squeeze, I am eternally grateful for you. Without your constant support, I would be suffering in my jocks big time.

Warren, mate, thanks for all your help in the kitchen, riffing on recipes with me, you're a dead-set bloody legend.

To Izzy, Clive and Adam, as always, thanks for letting me chuck a mono on the book bicycle again, I appreciate your encouragement greatly.

I have to of course give a huge shout-out to my incredibly talented dad for showing me heaps of cool tricks in the kitchen over the years; yours will always be the best food I've ever eaten in my life.

A big love ya to my beautiful friends as well, who have let me relentlessly shove food in their faces over the years and said such nice things about it.

To my management and booking team of Tom, Andrew and Julie, thanks for having my back and riding this crazy COVID entertainment train with me.

Last of all, thanks to you: the reader, the fan, the champion, as without you there wouldn't be any of this cool shit. Whether you've been with me from the boat show days or are a new listener, I love ya guts, thanks for your support. You're a bloody champion.